BOYS WILL BE MEN

By Richard A. Hawley

Hail University! A Century of University School Life.
University School Press, 1990.
Mr. *Chips Redux/Miss Dove Redivivus: In Praise of the
Teaching Life.* University School Press, 1988.
The Big Issues in the Passage to Adulthood. Walker and
Co., 1987.
Seeing Things: A Chronicle of Surprises. Walker and
Co., 1987.
Drugs and Society: Responding to an Epidemic. Walker
and Co., 1987.
St. Julian. Bits Press, 1987.
A *School Answers Back.* American Council on Drug
Education, 1984.
The Headmaster's Papers. Eriksson, 1983. Bantam,
1984. Revised Edition, Eriksson, 1992.
*The Purposes of Pleasure: A Reflection on Youth and
Drugs.* Independent School Press, 1983.
With Love to My Survivors. Cleveland State University
Poetry Center, 1982.

BOYS WILL BE MEN
Masculinity in Troubled Times

By
Richard A. Hawley

Introduction by Ron Powers

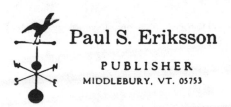

Paul S. Eriksson
PUBLISHER
MIDDLEBURY, VT. 05753

10 9 8 7 6 5 4 3 2 1

Library of Congress Cataloguing-in-Publication Data

Hawley, Richard A.
    Boys will be men: masculinity in troubled times / by Richard A.
Hawley; introduction by Ron Powers.
        p. cm.
    Includes bibliographical references and index.
    ISBN 0-8397-1193-X: $19.95
    1. Masculinity   (Psychology) 2. Men—
Psychology.   3. Masculinity
    (Psychology)—History.   4. Men—Psychology—History.   I. Title.
    BF692.5.H38 1993
155.3'32—dc20   93-6870
                                                              CIP

For Molly

What a piece of work is a man! how noble in
reason! how infinite in faculty! in form and moving
how express and admirable! in action how like an
angel! in apprehension how like a god! the beauty
of the world! the paragon of animals! And yet, to me,
what is this quintessence of dust?

—Hamlet, II, ii.

CONTENTS

INTRODUCTION

Some of the most amazing daylight in America spills onto the meadows of the Green Mountains in northern Vermont on cloudless evenings in August. It is a green-golden light that seems to burn all the way from a prior century, for it has the effect, upon the people whom it touches, of lifting them out of all the trivializing context of their times — credit cards, fitness machines, fashionable irony — and restoring them, for a few backlit moments, to a harmony with Arcadian place: a luminous arc of mowed field, a low stone wall, a scattering of Adirondack chairs. I know Richard Hawley best in this light, and I trust that it will not seem sentimental to introduce him in its clarifying glow, because I am certain that it is the light he uses to write by.

The particular place I speak of is the campus of the Bread Loaf Writers' Conference above Ripton, Vermont. Here, for the past several summers, I have watched Richard brilliantly and with unfailing sympathy analyze the prosewriting of his students, and here I have heard him read aloud from the astonishing manuscript that now appears in its proper book form. Richard Hawley, I have concluded, not only has bent this timeless light to his literary purposes; he has traced it to its source.

The aura of a slightly prior time is all about him: in his vocation as headmaster (of Cleveland's University School); in his dress and appearance (carelessly correct V-neck sweaters and Oxford shirts; an annoyingly gallant profile anchored by the sort of chin not commonly seen after 1923); and certainly in the unhesitant moral inquiry that underlies every sentence he sets to paper.

The aura is apt; Hawley the writer and the man is a magnificent retrograde. His great subjects are the dogged reach toward nobility in a case-hardened world, and its frequent concomitant, the great descending sorrow. His milieu is the ordinary but consecrated life. He is interested in duty (and the price that duty exacts among the dutiful); in honor; in laughter directed against the sorrow, and in the individual human character transfigured, not to stereotype but to archetype. Threading through all these concerns, but never insistent, is Hawley's sense of the numinous, his suspicion that the ordinary may be invisibly embraced by the divine.

These are risky themes in any age; they can easily seem cloying, or fraudulent. But this is not any age; this is the 20th century's close, the *fin* to *fin* all *siècles:* a time when American fiction has grown fashionably benumbed and self-referencing; biography, punitive and voyeuristic; nonfiction, infected with the processed cant of various "movements," and all discourse sealed in the industrial-strength prophylaxis of rote irony. ("What has happened to speech?" wonders a typically reasonable Hawley character. "Without clear, logical speech, everything goes—writing, even thought.") Set in this ratcheted context, Richard Hawley's themes are not risky so much as they are museum pieces.

Until, that is, they reach the light—Hawley's particular clarifying light.

His first novel, *The Headmaster's Papers* (Eriksson, 1983), gave us the exquisitely etched John Greeve, that civilized steward of the Wells School, eroding on his plinth, a dutiful, bereft man. Headmaster Greeve is not Headmaster Hawley; but like Hawley, he takes his moral illumination from a prior time. He performs his increasingly painful and frustrating ablutions according to a rapidly receding gentleman's code: common justice and civility and accumulated judgment based on immersion in a place.

Greeve's code stands in stubborn relief against the encircling forces of educators as social engineers, trustees as corporate determinists and students as experiments in unrestrained personal license. (Greeve's own son seems to have been a casualty of the latter.) The new forces prevail, as they must, and Greeve's fate is defeat, demise.

Except not so, because Hawley has preserved the soul of John Greeve for us by the radiance of language—Greeve's language. In the measured, exacting cadences of Greeve's "papers," his correspondences and poems and remarks to the students; in Greeve's constant unstressed appeal to everyone's better judgment, Hawley has implanted the foundations of a philosophic system. As we respond to that system through our empathy toward Greeve, we all become executors of Greeve's code.

Later, in an elegant nonfiction work, he throws a piercing shaft of light into his own past. *Seeing Things: A Chronicle of Surprises* (Walker, 1987), draws closer to the special idea that Hawley explores fully in the present book. This is the idea of childhood as a profound phase of life *on its own terms,* and not simply in relation to commercialized irony or nostalgia, on the one extreme, or the benumbed formulations of "child-care experts" on the other.

To be a child, as Hawley sumptuously reminds us, is to cross constantly between intense, elemental reality and the mythic. At age nine, he is sitting at the foot of a great elm tree in the town park with his friend Cyrus, a religious boy tortured by the mysteries of his developing sexuality. At this moment, the child Hawley is intensely aware of the moment, of the *facts* of the moment: the elm's exposed roots, the billowing cumulus clouds that have brought the blue sky to life, the wind flattening his and Cyrus's hair. In this instant of indisputable reality, Cyrus suddenly blurts: "God's right here."

It is in this instant that Hawley learns how to pray:

"God," I said, "I love you."
I was so happy. Something was lost—what?

It was myself. Everything I was, everything I thought I had made of myself was gone, behind me, blown away with the wind. I was simply aware, watching myself at the base of the tree, as if from high in the sky, that it had happened. It had finally happened. I was nine years old, barely awake, unschooled, undisciplined, far, far from good, but this great connectedness, this opening up had happened.

And now in green and golden light comes this capstone, this wise, original and gloriously truthful book.

Boys Will be Men joins an unruly conversation-in-progress in this culture; a conversation that has grown so polemic, so pre-formulated and so poisonously shrill on all sides that it will be a wonder, frankly, if this quiet book can make itself audible for a moment or two in the terrible din. It should. The conversation in question is about childhood, but it has grown all incoherent with an admixture of "gender politics," and "the inner child," and condom-distribution, and the permissible level of profanity in kid-karate movies, and whether teens understand the "irony" of cop-killer rap lyrics; and generally, the conversation is an hysterical mess.

Richard Hawley brings to this confusion the clarifying balm of storytelling. His subjects are the boys he has known as a headmaster, but the enfolding notion is *boy* as an archetypal idea. The stories he tells about boys here are true stories, in both the literal and the mythic sense of truth: Literal in that they are products of Hawley's unusual gift of *witness,* his prodigious power of attention to particulars of speech, dress, habit, ritual and the concealed narratives of daily life in the enclave of a boys' school. And mythic in that he illuminates this personal witness with the old light of civilized inquiry, from Genesis through Shakespeare on down through Freud and (we're near the far edge of civilization now) Iron John.

What emerges, for the reader (besides the sheer pleasure of good language) is a sequence of rekindlings — startling, often exhilarating, recognitions of insights once held about boys, but then meekly abandoned or pounded into deadness by the drumbeat of coarse stereotype, strident accusation, or mere merchandising.

I have sat in audiences that have erupted in sustained, cathartic laughter as Richard has read passages about boys in comic interludes. (His vignette in which a soccer coach and one of his struggling charges perfect an on-field vaudeville routine has left listeners limp.) A moment or two later, that same audience will have fallen pensively silent as Hawley has shifted to an accounting of boys in trouble; helpless boys; evil boys; dead boys.

The thrust of Hawley's witness is steadfastly, and unpolemically, hopeful. I recall a moment of my own rekindling. It burst forth from a typically understated passage from this book — the one in which Hawley dwells on the characteristics of first love. He proposes that, counter to the prevailing stereotype in Hollywood teen-buddy movies, in which boys are "leeringly preoccupied with sexual conquest," boys in fact tend to be touchingly romantic when stricken deeply by a girl.

In a wash of epiphany, I realized not only that Hawley was right, but that I had succumbed to the pandemic stereotype—*even as it affected my own memory*. I recalled, for the first time in more than a generation, the aching altruism of my own first love. Hawley had honored that memory more scrupulously even than I.

Perhaps Richard's work is understood best in relation to that *de rigueur* American literary stance, irony, a quality I've alluded to above. The writer Paul Fussell has made a wintry proposition, near the beginning of his towering work, *The Great War and Modern Memory* (Oxford), regarding 20th-century consciousness: "I am saying that there seems to be one dominating form of modern understanding; that is is essentially ironic; and that it originates largely in the application of mind and memory to the events of the Great War."

Perhaps this is so, and we are the colder for it. Hawley's work is singularly free from the tyranny of irony. (He doesn't deny its function; he simply allots it, as he allots every other value, its proper weight.) It is in this freedom that his writing most clearly reflects that "prior" light. It recalls the staunch optimism of the 19th-century British headmaster—Matthew Arnold's father Thomas comes to mind—an optimism itself illuminated by the teachings of Christ and Aristotle.

In liberating boys from corrosive irony on the one hand and from sterile formulations on the other, Richard Hawley has done nothing less, in this fine book, than restore childhood to us all. I understand my own sons better for having seen them in its light.

—Ron Powers

SOMETHING WRONG:
A Prefatory Note on Gender

Not even a casual reader can have failed to notice the phenomenal profusion of printed material about gender that continues to appear in the waning years of this century. It is no mere coincidence that so much published speculation has been accompanied by a growing loss of conviction about what it means to be a man or a woman.

The truth of the matter is that nobody really, or naturally, likes to think about gender. Thinking about gender is irritating in the same way thinking about breathing or the beating of our hearts is irritating. We don't have or acquire a gender; we *are* gendered. In our deepest beings, from the first, we are male or female. We discover this fact; we do not invent it. When we think about gender, that thinking is gendered.

We think analytically and prescriptively about

breathing when something goes wrong with our lungs or with the air. At present, something is obviously wrong with gender, with gender relations in particular, to the extent that widespread educational and political reforms are being sought.

It is not easy to generalize effectively about the gender concerns of the past half century. Nevertheless, it seems that one of two sets of circumstances must be true. The first—massively in the ascendant among feminists and depth psychologists—is that what is wrong in gender relations has been wrong for a very long time. Not at the dawn of humankind, but shortly afterwards, some kind of trick or power play was carried out in human communities nearly everywhere resulting in male domination and female subordination. At the level of household, clan, village, and polity, men determined the living and working arrangements in ways that maximized their preferences. Religious systems, legal codes, artistic and historical records were designed by men to support their political position. The result is what many now call generically the Patriarchy, and those who think this way want to hasten the Patriarchy's demise, in favor of a new order characterized by less brutality, more nurturance, and gender equity.

The second alternative is less popular but very possibly true. It brings together such unlikely theorists as Ivan Illich and G.K. Chesterton. According to this view, there was no original trick or male power play. Political and economic arrangements throughout history reflect the innate and distinctive characteristics of humankind, of gendered men and women. The historical record will reveal brutal and intolerable gender relations, and it will also reveal elegant and mutually respectful ones. But regardless of the quality and variety of their behavior over time, men and women have acted in the natural modalities of their respective genders. What is currently wrong has occurred fairly recently. Conditions of modern production have coerced men and women and children to live and work and school themselves in ways that do not allow them to realize their full humanity. Husbands and wives are alienated and distanced from one another; parents are alienated and distanced from children. Men and women are encouraged to be economically interchangeable parts. Work itself has become abstract and ultimately incomprehensible. The basis for loving, sustained relationships — for families — has disappeared. In this modern arrangement, the very idea of gender, of innate gender, is a threat. There are commercial inducements to make a "unisex," to "blend" the genders, to make them equal in value, to make them meaningless.

Seen in either of these two ways, contemporary civilization has a gender problem. Of the two views sketched above, the second seems to me more compelling. For one thing, it provides a good explanation for why people have begun to espouse the first view. Prickly and even hopeless as discussions of gender issues may presently seem, there is perhaps some consolation if one·is willing to assume a longer historical perspective. If gender really is deep and inalienable in our nature, it won't sit back quietly for long — much less disappear — if it is normed or legislated against. Like one of its offspring, sexuality, gender has the capacity to make fools out of individuals and of whole societies who get it wrong — either by undervaluing it, overvaluing it, or negating it.

Getting gender right requires less judgment right now than it does honest observation. The good news here is that we are loaded with evidence. Neither gender, as the following chapters suggest, has a reliable record of defining the other. This is not to say males and females cannot understand one another. I believe that, within limits, they can and do. It is to say, however, that males and females cannot understand one another in the same way they understand themselves.

Over the past quarter century, women have spoken more often and more loudly about gender, principally their own, than men have done, although lately there has been a flurry of "about men" treatises, seemingly written in compensation. Therein may lie their weakness: they seek mainly to compensate, and they propose a compensatory, "corrected" man, a man who regrets the Patriarchy and wants to start again in a nicer way. He tends to be agreeable, but not convincing. He may be not quite a man.

This book is written out of the conviction that it is possible to locate real men and even real manhood. Amidst their partially realized, brutish, politically corrected, and otherwise befogged fellows, real men abound in the historical and literary record. They are still afoot. Many of them, I believe, are boys.

BOYS WILL BE MEN

ONE

Being Male

So God created man in his own image; in the image of
God he created him; male and female he created them.

— Genesis 1:27,28

Then the Lord God formed a man from the dust of the
ground and breathed into his nostrils the breath
of life. Thus the man became a living creature.

— Genesis 2:7

The feminist momentum through the past cen-
tury's politics, art, and scholarship has left in its wake a
surprising void. Western peoples find themselves without a clear, common understanding of what it means to
be male. It is of course possible to define modern males
as an accretion of qualities — i.e., dangerous aggression,
sexual domination, insensitivity — unacceptable to feminists. To the extent "negative" definitions like these

3

are accepted, males begin to compensate by self-conscious attempts to behave in a more prescribed "feminine" manner, or perhaps, persuaded by so-called New Age psychological attitudes, attempt to "get in touch with" and express the "feminine side" of themselves. The latter tendency is based on the assumption of deep psychological androgyny, a condition both men and women are urged to recognize and express in order to realize their true nature.

Missing, of course, in these revised constructions of masculinity is any positive, sustaining masculine principle. The New Age man or the man merely acceptable to feminists is a compensation, not an inherently valuable being. What is male about him is a problem, or at least a potential problem, and the corrective is applied or liberated femininity.

MALES AS IMPOSTORS: The Freudian Legacy

The habit of defining masculinity in compensatory or negative terms can hardly, in fairness, be attributed to modern feminists. Freud himself based his theory of male psychological development on a series of culturally unacceptable and physically unattainable desires infants are assumed to feel for their parents. Accordingly, every infant boy is unconsciously the Oedipus of Sophocles' tragedy.[1] He wants to possess his mother physically, to have her solely to himself. He also simultaneously fears and resents his (enormous) father and would like to eliminate him. The infant's tension over these anxious desires is brought to a crisis when, through anatomical observation or perhaps bio-genetic memory, he understands that his penis could be removed by his father-competitor. Feeding this cas-tration dread is the "proof" that others — females — have apparently had their penises removed. The infant male's unbearable tension over these Oedipal feelings is resolved by a number of psychological adaptations, or defenses. For instance, in the complex's heterosex-ual resolution, the boy vents his desire for his mother by idealizing her permanently but unconsciously as an "object choice," the model for all amorous female at-tractions to come. The fear and hostility felt for the father are expressed in a cathartic "identification" with him; in effect, Freud maintained, the boy uncon-sciously determines that he will overcome his father by incorporating him — an act, in Freud's words, of "psy-chic cannibalism."

In the Freudian scheme, a child's assumption of psychological masculinity is an imposture, motivated by unbearable dread. As the imposture becomes con-firmed by cultural reinforcements — that is, as junior is recognized as a chip off the old block — the identifica-tion with the boy's father, or some father figure, be-comes locked into his mature personality. Grown up, the counterfeit father in turn terrifies his own sons to the point that they identify with him; thus is mas-culinity transmitted through the ages.

Freud's disciple, Karen Horney, agreed that early masculine development is shaped by dread, but she detected pre-Oedipal forces at work. Long before he has recognized his father as a competitor and sex-ual assailant, the infant male is pitted in a problematic opposition to his mother.[2] In Nancy Chodorow's words:

> The mother initially has complete power over the child's satisfaction of needs and first forbids instinctive activities . . . This creates enormous anxiety in the child. Fear of the father is not so threatening. It develops later in life, and as a result of specific processes which the boy is more "aware" that he is experiencing.[3]

As Horney, Chodorow, and other psychoanalytic feminists construct him, the infant boy's problems with his mother are serious. Moreover, his solutions to these problems have profoundly negative effects on both himself and the world's women.

The boy's dread of his mother exceeds infinitely his dread of his father, because his very life emerges from and, for a time, depends on her. She is his foremost nurturer as well as the agent of all his fears and dissatisfactions. He has issued from her very flesh, he needs her, but he increasingly realizes that he is not like her; the very source of his well-being is alien. At the time of this preconceptual, all-being realization on the part of the infant boy, older men are not much help. They are not, either in the remote past or now, likely to be the primary nurturers. To the contrary, in the industrialized west, fathers and other men contribute increasingly little to child-rearing at any stage of development; conditions of work and other deep habits tend to keep men out of the house and out of their infant offsprings' ken. Thus, the besetting male crisis is not what to do about a threatening giant father, but rather what to make of oneself when there is only a giant mother on the scene. Mother is every male's life support, lover, and human model—but he is not like her; he is something else. But what?

The male's two greatest existential problems, then, are what to make of mother and what to make of himself. Horney maintains that mothers, and by extension all females, become of necessity objects of masculine dread. Harpies, sirens, witches, whirlpools, caves, abysses, night, and death itself come to symbolize the consuming, ominous side of mother in the male infant's mind. Since there can be no psychological ease for him until he resolves this dread, the boy opts for one of two alternatives. He either idealizes and adores the mother (and by extension women in general), or he debases and abuses them. Adoration elevates the mother figure into beneficent harmlessness. Debasement devalues her into contemptible harmlessness. Either way, the developing male gains psychological control, although at the cost of distorting the reality and value of females. If older males are absent or only glancingly present while the child is identifying himself as a male, he will very likely exaggerate his tendency to adore or to debase females. He may also deny the very existence of feminine qualities in himself and in the world about him. Exaggerated, inflated tendencies to aggression, loudness, and swagger may help differentiate him from the mother he consciously knows he is not but who, he fears unconsciously, may reassume him into herself. Clearly recognizable phases of exaggeratedly masculine—that is, unmotherly, unfeminine—behavior can be seen in the childhood experience of most boys and many girls. And of course the tendency may persist past childhood. There is Rambo, also Rimbaud.

Horney's construction of masculine development is, like Freud's, thoroughly negative in its consequences. Men are fated to distort the nature of women by either overvaluing or undervaluing them, and because their misunderstanding is a necessary condition of their psychological security, males must usurp political power and cultural influence in order to legitimize their distorted views. The accrued losses to females are enormous, spanning all of history and, for all we know, prehistory. But for all of that, if Horney is correct, males may have suffered even greater losses: they appear to have, so long as they are born of women, no positive identity whatsoever. Their life's course is propelled by a desperate impulse not to be their mothers or to be consumed by them.

On many counts, the way Horney and other contemporary feminist thinkers have constructed the masculine condition is troubling to males. It is a view that challenges the very basis for males' traditional, generally tacit claims on material resources and to political power. Deeper still, males are invited to consider a chilling possibility: that there is nothing distinctive, nothing substantial, nothing essential to their natures. The machismo, the will to power, and all manner of other exaggerated tendencies may be the only maleness there is; masculinity may be all compensation.

CORRECTED MALES: The Jungian Legacy

A number of late twentieth century thinkers, all men and led by such prominent Jungians as Robert Johnson, Thomas Moore, James Hillman, and Robert Bly,[4] maintain that masculine qualities are both genuine and essential. They too see modern man caught in a predicament, but his problem is not that he has a bad nature or that he is nature-less; the problem, rather, is that part of his true nature has been suppressed by contemporary culture. A deep, primitive, inalienable virility lies ominously in the unconscious of every male. In the late twentieth century, well-intentioned but futile gestures on the part of educated western men have surfaced in response to the feminist critique of masculinity. As Robert Bly, one of the founders of what has become known as the men's movement, summarizes the situation, the emphasis on personal liberation stressed in the '60s counter-culture allowed men to break out of stereotypical male behavior. Accordingly, some men chose to accept more responsibility for household work, to participate more actively in nurturing small children, to be more emotionally expressive, to admit not liking football, etc. Getting emotionally closer to females and to one's own "female side" was, Bly maintains, genuinely liberating and deepening to the man who made such gestures. But the liberation came at a cost. For while new, more aggressive women were energized by the new, more accommodating men, the men found themselves enervated by their transformation.

The new man—whom Bly has labeled "the soft man"—is in fact depressed. When such men enroll in one of Bly's all-male therapeutic retreats, they arrive psychologically bruised, often weeping. Bly does not apply the "soft man" label in a pejorative sense. There is some merit to softness, but the soft approach to masculine life is insufficient for self-realization. The soft man has fallen out of touch with his deep maleness: a phallic, pre-civilized energy sometimes projected in symbolic form as a monster or giant.

Bly sees the soft man's predicament—and its resolution—in the Grimm tale of "Iron John" (sometimes "Iron Hans"). To summarize it briefly: a kingdom is troubled by the disappearance of hunters who enter a remote area of the royal forest. A stranger passing through learns of the problem and volunteers to help. When he enters the dangerous region, a great hand arises from out of a pond and pulls the stranger's dog down to the depths. The stranger then returns to the castle for help. With a number of volunteers, he drains the pond, bucketful by bucketful. At the bottom lies a reddish, rust-colored giant, covered with hair from head to toe. The giant, Iron John, is captured and carried back to the castle where he is displayed in a cage. One day soon after, the king's young son is playing nearby with his treasured golden ball. When the ball rolls within Iron John's grasp, he grabs it. To get the ball back, the boy is told he will have to hand over the key to the cage. Since the key lies under the mother's pillow, a deception is required of the boy. He secures the key while his parents are away and releases Iron John, but as the giant heads off to the forest, the boy hollers after him that his parents will be very angry when they realize what has happened. The giant agrees, and the two head off into the wilderness together. The youth returns to the civilized world and is periodically refortified by an Iron John experience.

The features of Iron John—hairiness, wetness, redness—are associated with primitive male sexuality: they are not easily acceptable, not nice. The pond, Bly suggests, is the subconscious mind, and emptying it bucket-by-bucket represents a patient, disciplined attempt to discover what lies "at the bottom."

The Iron John figure holds the developing boy's nature—the golden ball—in his menacing hands. By reconciling himself with the giant, the boy is reconciling himself with his complete nature. It is instructive that the boy must also use his wiles to secure the key to Iron John's cage from under his mother's pillow. The mother here is the obstacle to the boy's reconciliation with his own deep masculinity.

From the standpoint of civilization, community, and family, the "Iron John" tale is problematic. The lad and the giant coexist in an uneasy tension. Taken as a social formula, "Iron John" is regressive, a worrying return to the primitive. But from the individual male's standpoint, that return is healing and welcome. The boy becoming a man must remember that he is forceful. Being forceful and strong are his masculine birthright; it is civilization's job to educate him to the distinction between being strong and being destructive. It is civilization's job also to learn that the solution to civic and domestic violence is not to weaken men to the point that they cannot commit it.

While Bly and like-minded associates of the men's movement have identified a positive masculine need to regain strength and direction, some of the therapeutic measures they appear to endorse seem unlikely to achieve that end.[5] These measures have included intimate male-male disclosure in "support group" settings, healing rapprochement with fathers or father figures, the cultivation of "male mentors" or "male mothers" on the part of adolescents, and the enactment of primitive, earthy (but not violent or destructive) male bonding rituals. Whatever therapeutic outcomes, including positive ones, result from these kinds of men's movement activities, they are not notably masculine. Such activity is either directly parallel or structurally identical to the business of contemporary female groups.

MALES AS HERMAPHRODITES:
The Classical Tradition Gone Wrong

That self-proclaimed men's groups should lay stress on such traditionally feminine themes as nurturing—as opposed to, say, questing and conquering—is to some degree due to their assumption that men (and women) are psychologically androgynous, each person embodying mental characteristics of both genders. Outwardly and consciously people tend to express their biologically visible gender. Inwardly and unconsciously, the other gender presses for attention and expression. Freud and Jung both theorized extensively about psychological androgyny and drew biogenetic support from the fact that males and females bear attenuated or vestigial organs of the other gender: e.g., the male nipples, the female clitoris. Jung called the shadowy but ever-present gender-other the *anima* in males, the *animus* in females. The anima and animus are seen as unconscious motivators of conscious behavior, and they appear as shadowy presences in dreams and in artwork. They have desires and needs, which if repressed or slighted, unbalance the individual to the point of neurosis or worse.[6]

Whatever such concepts contribute to psychological understanding and to therapy, the presence of androgynous elements in the psyche does not indicate true androgyny—any more than the male nipple will yield milk. The classical Greeks, who introduced the idea of androgyny to the west, took the opposite view to Freud's and Jung's. In Plato's *Symposium*,[7] a charming myth is proposed by Aristophanes to account for gender differentiation and heterosexual attraction. In it, members of a race of spherical, two-sexed beings are cut in half, so that the unity of masculinity and femininity is severed, as happens when an original hermaphrodite is severed. The story is actually more complicated than this. Aristophanes describes three original, spherical genders, male, female, and hermaphrodite. When each is severed, it seeks its other half. Severed males seek males, severed females seek females, and severed hermaphrodites seek their missing halves. In consequence, the severed halves of the former hermaphrodite—man and woman—are fated to pursue each other in order to bring about a satisfying reunion. The point is that, while each gender seeks the other with the aim of recreating a unity, males and females are differentiated; they are not androgynous. Truly androgynous characters, such as the blind hermaphrodite Tiresias who pops up in Sophocles' *Oedipus the King* and in a number of other myths and legends, is not an ideal person, although he possesses prophetic visions. Greek men and women were not enjoined to become like Tiresias. By and large he/she is a dreadful person, a freak.

Assuming that men are psychologically androgynous may well, instead of deepening masculine understanding, distort male experience beyond recognition. Nor is it certain what male-male encounter groups, as structured by current men's-movement leaders, will contribute to a clear definition of maleness or to the well-being of males. While promising things might be said of assembling males to share male experience and insights, there is also something inherently limiting in the process. There is a passivity and a self-consciousness to men's groups discussing manhood that would not be true of men's groups hunting buffalo or playing football. Male bonding, expressing male exuberance and joy, and fortifying masculine resolves, will more likely be experienced by a vigorous men's softball team than by a men's support group. The softball team has male experiences; the "support group" has an experience of a kind, but it is a reflective, analytic step removed from dynamic, in-this-world maleness.

SAD NEW AGE MEN

The New Age man is one who has been badly bruised at the hands of late-twentieth-century culture. The proposed remedy is a kind of therapeutic male solidarity—a kinder, gentler solidarity, not the politically incorrect kind provided by college fraternities, men's clubs, and corner taverns. The New Age man accepts axiomatically the feminist assessment of his nature. He learns that his existential shortcomings should not be compensated for by exaggerated, aggressive behavior. In this regard, he realizes he is dangerous. He and his kind are inclined to political and economic gender discrimination, date rape, wife beating, and other forms of misogyny.

The New Age man does not like these qualities in himself and in others. He would honestly like to do better, to be a good man, even to be a hero. But in the New Age, the old heroes—Alexander, Caesar, Charlemagne, Napoleon—are exposed as flawed, dangerous characters. The New Age man knows his strength, his sexual urges, and his every appetite are suspect. His impulse to set off on his own, to separate himself from groups and institutions, to withhold his emotions and thoughts, to be silent—these too reveal his inadequacy.

The New Age man is a corrected man. The previous model was chauvinist, misogynous, a menace. The corrected man is more sympathetic, more collaborative, more nurturing. He is more androgynous and thus more feminine.

The New Age man has turned away from what was definitively male in his father. In so doing, he may have forfeited his sons.

TWO

When Boys Take Off

Mama, don't let your babies grow up to be cowboys...
—Song, Willie Nelson

Masculinity is best understood as a trajectory. In literature it is described as a journey or quest. A young hero leaves home and hearth and takes off. The destination is profound, but uncertain. The hero, as Joseph Campbell has written, wears a thousand faces.[8] He is Odysseus bound for Troy, then bound for Ithaca. He is Telemachus in search of his father, young David on his way to the front to greet his brothers and challenge the Philistines. He is Percival in quest of the Grail message, Pip in pursuit of great expectations, Huck Finn gliding down the Mississippi. Sometimes the destination is profound, but certain: Icarus flying toward the sun, Christ agonizing toward Calvary. Arriving at the desti-

17

nation, achieving the mission is not the point; the point is the progress, out away from the source. The trajectory of that progress is masculinity.

The trajectory of masculinity is prefigured by the male's physical expulsion out into the world, then the drama of his infant experiences as he begins to conceive of his identity in relation to the mother from whose body he has issued and who is now sustaining his life. He cannot identify with her entirely because he is different from her, not just a separate being, but a different kind of being. The nature of other males, with whom he will become more familiar later, is at first remote and abstract.

The male trajectory begins with the first gesture of separation from the mother. This need to differentiate sets the boy on a life-long path of, literally, proving himself. This, Margaret Mead has suggested, he must achieve by doing things as opposed to merely being, which suffices for feminine identity.[9] In *The Second Sex*, Simone de Beauvoir reflects rather wistfully on the male's existential lot:

> The young boy, be he ambitious, thoughtless, or timid, looks toward an open future; he will be a seaman or an engineer, he will stay on the farm or he will go away to the city, he will see the world, he will get sick; he feels free, confronting a future in which the unexpected awaits him.[10]

Years before he will think realistically about seamanship or engineering, the infant male is fashioning an approach to physical space, to material objects, and to his immediate society. With increased conceptual and motor ability, his play begins to reveal distinctively masculine features. He thrusts himself and parts of himself boldly into surrounding space, testing previous boundaries, frequently intruding into other people's business. Erik Erikson has pointed out the tendencies, given common objects to play with, of boys to build towers and girls to build enclosures:

> The most significant sex difference was the tendency of boys to erect structures, buildings, towers, or streets. The girls tended to use the play table as the interior of a house, with simple, little, or no use of blocks.

> High structures, then, were prevalent in the configurations of the boys. But the opposite of elevation, i.e., downfall was equally typical for them: ruins or fallen down structures were exclusively found among boys.[11]

At each successive stage of infant development, as each successive body zone—oral, anal, genital—is trained and "socialized," the trajectory of male experience stands in clear relief. By the "phallic stage" of development (approximately the third to fifth year), boys are emphatically boys. Erikson observes:

> The ambulatory stage and that of infantile genitality add to the inventory of basic social modalities that of "making," first in the sense

of "being on the make." There is no simpler,
stronger word for it; it suggests pleasure in
attack and conquest; in the boy the emphasis
remains on phallic-intrusive modes . . .[12]

With respect to the defining characteristics of growing
boys, the western literary record and the psychoanalytic theory of child development could hardly be more
congruent. The myths of Phaeton and Icarus, the legends of young Alcibiades and Alexander—all suggest
the irrepressible thrust of masculine initiative.

FROM LITTLE FOOL TO TROUBLED HERO:
Percival's Story

A number of Jungian writers[13] have seen in the
Arthurian legend of Percival (or Parsifal) a complete
model of masculine development. The legend is
thought to transcend the medieval era in which it was
formally composed as well as the more remote eras
ascribed by warring scholarly camps as the source of
the legend. As a story which "anticipates psychic problems reaching so far into the future that it could not be
wholly comprehended by the medieval attitude,"[14] the
legend of Percival has been held up as an archetypal
map into maleness.

In his commentary on masculinity, *He!*, Jungian
scholar Robert Johnson proposes that the contours of
Percival's legend describe male psychology generally.
Like Percival, every surviving male passes from relative
innocence to experience, from impulsiveness to delib-

erate action. Like Percival, males are tested by the prevailing conventions of male culture. Like Percival, males must interact adaptively with a variety of women, and they must be sustained by a beckoning, transcendent sense of mission, or else they will turn inward in confusion and despair.

Percival's story is at once highly distinctive and broadly universal. Percival emerges into consciousness, into story, as a high-spirited little fool. He is unschooled, unsophisticated, a mama's boy. Apart from his precocious ability to sink hand-whittled javelins into targets, Percival has no special talent or genius. Yet he soon reveals himself as a possessor of unshakable determination.

An innocent and naive boy (etymologically, "Percival" and "Parsifal" mean "little fool") is brought up in rustic seclusion by a protective mother, Heart's Sorrow. Widowed by the death of her knight husband, she has also lost older sons to chivalric warfare. Hoping to spare her remaining child a similar fate, she retires with him to a forest. Here her plans are thwarted when the boy (as yet unnamed) meets a party of knights on the road. The child is so immediately taken with the sheen and beauty of their presence he mistakes them for angels. He cannot get enough of them, cannot satisfy his curiosity about them. Without a father to temper his enthusiasm, to forbid or to dissuade him, young Percival succeeds in having his way. He asks them endless foolish questions about their mounts and armor before the knights depart. Having learned, however, that knights are created by King Arthur at court, Percival is determined to leave home at once in pursuit of knighthood.

Accepting this inevitability, Percival's mother advises him carefully on the necessity of regular worship, although he has not yet seen a chapel, and of extreme courtesy to women. Outfitted with a new suit of peasant clothes and armed with a whittled javelin, Percival sets out on life's path astride the family nag, its tack improvised from sticks and twigs.

The youthful Percival is every boy. His heart's desire can be compromised by parental accommodations or it can be forcibly resisted, but it cannot be extinguished—without killing the boy himself. Every boy similarly longs to be a knight, a questing, adventuring, fully realized man. The social recognition of this psychological inevitability is seen in the way boys' play is culturally accommodated and commercially supported. Whole industries are organized to supply boys with knightly props: in one era cowboy boots and pearl-handled cap pistols, in another space suits and simulated laser guns. Whatever the knightly "style"—Robin Hood's, Sir Galahad's, The Three Musketeers', The Lone Ranger's, or Luke Skywalker's—every boy recognizes it on sight. At a later stage of male play, athletic conventions and athletic gear may beckon with a resonant power.

In fact, the style of knighthood, even the exaggerated style, arouses a boy's spirit long before he is able to imagine knightly substance. The knight's true substance, his virtue, is an abstract quality, not yet conceivable to a developing boy. But style—a knight's trappings—are something else. From the instant Percival beheld the five knights—angels—he wanted to look like one, to dress like one, to have what they had.

Now on his way and happening upon a tent he mistakes for a chapel, Percival intrudes into the presence of a knight's lady. Thoroughly misunderstanding his mother's instructions and the lady's situation, Percival eats her food for his supper and takes away her ring.

Percival proceeds to Arthur's court, in fact rides his mount into Arthur's hall and nearly collides with him. Arthur has been distracted by an outrageous insult to Guinevere and himself tendered by an audacious Red Knight, now lurking nearby awaiting Arthur's answer to his challenge. Percival is led to believe he can win knighthood if he vanquishes the Red Knight, but before he sets out to do so, a maiden of the court who has been mute for years laughs at Percival. This fulfills a prophecy that the girl would not laugh until she beheld the greatest knight in the world. Furious at this seemingly impossible turn of events, one of Arthur's knights, Sir Kay, berates the girl and tosses a palace fool, who has interpreted the girl's outburst, into the fire.

Percival proceeds to locate the Red Knight who shows nothing but irritation to the unpresentable lad. At one point the Red Knight knocks Percival to the ground with the blunt end of his lance. In response, Percival, with a much practiced gesture, hurls his pointed stick through the Red Knight's eye, killing him. Percival falls immediately upon the dead knight's armor, but he can't figure out how it works, how to get it off or how to put it on. Ultimately he has to rely on assistance from an instructed page. Now an outwardly fearsome Red Knight himself, Percival sets out in his

new armor on a powerful new mount. He is transformed—but not completely. He has donned the new
armor over his mother's homespun, and, as Robert
Johnson points out,[15] this represents every boy's reticence to abandon altogether and too quickly his
mother's hold on his nature.

The mother's influence must be shed, but it must
be shed gradually. Because Percival's mother was good,
her influence on him was good. He is obliged to discard
it not because of its goodness, but because it will not
work for him as a man. Even her reasonable and loving
instructions to worship regularly and to treat women
courteously are imperfectly communicated. This is not
Heart's Sorrow's fault, for what can she know about
how a boy learns? Because Percival is a good boy, he
takes his mother's instructions to heart, but he botches
them badly in the knight's lady's tent. He must be
instructed further, by a male mentor.

Percival dwells for a time with a mentor, Gornemans, who instructs him in the ways of true chivalry.
Every boy seeks and needs a male mentor, whether
teacher, coach, or boss. Gornemans serves in this critical role for Percival. He is not Percival's father, although he instructs the boy in a way that would certainly have pleased the boy's late father. He inspires
Percival to seek life's supreme spiritual goal, the Grail.
To do this he must be able to resist the urgings of the
supreme natural appetite: sexual desire. He is advised
neither to seduce, nor to be seduced. He is also instructed in a seemingly minor virtue: reticence. He is to
stop doing impulsive things and asking impulsive questions. Attending to this point of masculine style is the

source of Percival's greatest difficulties later, when he refrains from asking after the Grail objects. Percival leaves Gornemans' court (although the older man would have preferred that he stay longer) not only a wiser, but a more manly man. No longer does he wear his mother's homespun beneath his armor.

He is now ready to meet the human other: woman. Blanche Fleur is perfectly attractive to Percival, and he is ready for her in a way he was obviously not for the knight's lady in the tent. Blanche Fleur is in distress; moreover, her story suggests that distress is inherent to her condition as an independent, unwed woman. However much the damsel-in-distress motif stands in tense opposition to twentieth century construction of super-adequate women, this is plainly Blanche Fleur's state when Percival meets her, and her distress is inseparable from her nature and thus from Percival's attraction to her.

It is Blanche Fleur's need that draws Percival into her presence—not her beauty, sex appeal, or accomplishments. She is not like Percival; she is not a likely friend or peer. She is a lady, capable of conception, nurture, and of all manner of feminine arts. She could technically retain her femininity intact if she submitted to the repulsive suitor who is laying siege to her estate, but to do so without love would devalue everything: femininity and life itself. Percival's knightly conduct requires him to risk great danger and discomfort, even to risk his life, in order to meet Blanche Fleur's need.

This need and Percival's duty are natural complements. But as Gornemans has taken pains to caution him, Percival's duty could be undermined by certain distractions, also natural. Being wholly feminine, Blanche Fleur is attractive to, and also powerfully attracted by, Percival. She seeks him out one night in his bed chamber. They exchange vows and share a single embrace, brow to brow, toe to toe, until morning.

Aware now that he has neglected his mother, Percival departs Blanche Fleur, although she has become imprinted on his heart as the ideal lover-mate. He is in no way dissatisfied with her or tired of her. He ventures beyond her because his nature requires it. Saving and joining Blanche Fleur are part of Percival's nature, but not all of it. There is in addition the Grail to be beheld and understood.

On his journey he comes to a river where two fishermen direct him to a nearby castle. Shrouded by a strange, unworldly atmosphere, this castle, though near at hand, is difficult for Percival to locate. When he does arrive, he is graciously received and outfitted in scarlet. His host, a crippled and ailing Fisher King, presents Percival with a special sword which, if broken, can only be repaired by its maker. This puzzling presentation is followed by a silent procession of Grail objects: a lad bearing a bleeding lance, followed by two others carrying lighted candles in silver candelabra, a maiden bearing the Grail, which emanates a light so brilliant it extinguishes the candles, and another maiden bearing a silver carving platter. Percival wishes to ask about these things, but, mindful of Gornemans' advice, remains silent.

While the meaning of the Grail has been interpreted in a variety of different ways, certain features of the symbol stand out clearly. "Grail" derives from latinate words for bowl or platter. In Christian tradition, the

Holy Grail is the vessel Joseph of Arimathea used to collect the blood from the crucified Christ's body after his side was pierced by a Roman lance. The Grail is also associated with the dish from which Christ served the eucharistic meal at the Last Supper. In both instances, the Grail is understood to dispense the very substance of Christ, Son of God and Son of man. By fusing an element of the first eucharist, a symbolic offering of Christ's bodily substance, with a dish used to preserve the actual blood from his wounds, the Grail symbol promises an especially powerful transmission of holy spirit. The Grail's many benefactions are summarized by Jung and Von Franz:

> It dispenses material food according to taste and imparts spiritual solace. It preserves youth and generally maintains life. In one instance it heals knights wounded in battle. It radiates light and a sweet fragrance, it rejoices the heart, and whoever sees it can commit no sin that day. It discriminates between good and evil. To the unbaptised it remains invisible. It makes known the will of God by means of writing which appears upon it. Only he who is destined by heaven and whose name is written thereon can find the Grail. Nor does it allow its defender to have any loves other than the one the Grail prescribes for him.[16]

To seek nourishment from the Grail, as Percival does, is to seek a man's true, revealed nature. The quest itself is worldly—that is, it takes place in the material world of living people, friends, foes, parents, children, lovers, animals, food and drink, mortal challenges. But the realization of the quest—partaking of the Grail— transcends the world. The Grail quest, the masculine trajectory, is through the world to what lies beyond it. It is a trajectory of ultimate ascent. James Hillman locates this masculine tendency to ascend in the psychological archetype *puer eternus:*

> Because of this vertical direct access to the spirit, this immediacy where vision of goal and goal itself are one, winged speed, haste— even the short cut—are imperative. The puer cannot do with indirection, with timing and patience. It knows little of the seasons and of waiting.[17]

When Percival passes into the enchanted realm of the Fisher King's Court, he is overcome by its mystery. None of its conventions are explained to him. When the procession of dazzling Grail objects passes through the room, he is speechless; rather, he holds his tongue. What was he afraid of? Of breaking the worldly code he had learned from Gornemans? Or of something deeper: transcendence itself, the end of the worldly life? Because of his reticence, Percival is all but expelled from the Fisher King's court, never, in some accounts, to return.

The following morning Percival awakes to find himself alone in the palace. As he departs the empty estate on his charger, the drawbridge is drawn up abruptly behind him. As soon as he makes his solitary exit from the Fisher King's castle, he receives one mortifying bit of news after another. Whereas his life had heretofore been propelled into an irresistible future, he is now summoned to various aspects of his past.

Percival's progress slows to a halt. Drops of goose blood staining the snow before him send him into deep reverie. He yearns for Blanche Fleur, white and pure as the snow, but it is unclear why the drops of blood stimulate his longing. Perhaps they remind him of the drops of blood he saw issuing from the Grail lance: one of the marvels after which he has failed to inquire. The conjunction of these two symbols stops him still.

Percival knows no peace even when he has taken his place among the knights of Arthur's round table. A hideous damsel uncannily singles him out for rebuke, reminding him of his failure to ask after the Grail and of the misfortune that will now follow. Percival's renewed commitment to seek the Grail and not to rest in the same place for two consecutive nights until he achieves it lacks the hopeful and purposeful thrust of his original, less self-conscious quest. The difficulty in ending Percival's story may lie in the nature of male experience. If the masculine trajectory really is an ascent, up and out of this world, there can be no coherent, worldly closure to the story. One either ascends miraculously as Jesus did after the resurrection, or one ends his days, confused, incomplete, seasoned perhaps, but weary of the world. Odysseus, having returned to Ithaca and slain his rival suitors, is reunited at last with Penelope and Telemachus. But then what?

The literary record suggests a conclusion so discouraging that few writers have cared to dwell on it: men do not live happily ever after. If they are reflective at all, they end their days like King Lear: a self-proclaimed "poor, infirm, weak, and despised old man" (III, ii, 20); or perhaps like Conrad's Mr. Kurtz, in febrile decline in the heart of darkness ("the horror, the horror"); or like Hemingway's old man at sea, Santiago, struggling hopelessly against all the elements to reel in a fish that would sustain him, in the end trailing only its ravaged skeleton into port.

STORIES WITHOUT END:
Males and the Problem of Mortality

In the canon of western literature, there are few stories of men who find wisdom and fulfillment in maturity or old age. Directed, satisfying experience belongs to youth, or at least to those committed to youthful quests. Maturity carries with it compromise, error, failure, loss, and suffering. Alexander, the boy-conqueror of the world, ends his life at thirty-three, friendless, feverish, and deranged. Caesar's once-triumphant course leads through conflict and calamity to public slaughter, the drama of which continues unabated through the ages: Lincoln, Gandhi, Martin Luther King. Camelot is not to last, not finally to be.

The satisfying, the (literally) arresting male stories tell of youth facing the challenges of youth. It is not merely for narrative convenience that so many enduring male stories conclude in the hero's fall from grace or early death. Hamlet's clear-eyed realization of the inherent misery of his condition as a son could not be assuaged by his living longer. What could an old Hamlet be, other than Lear?

Romeo flew to his Juliet like a moth to flame. Again, there is no plausible "happily ever after" for such a lover, not in Verona, not in Mantua; practically sustaining that pitch of feeling over time would inevitably diminish and kill it. The prince winning the princess and half her kingdom is, like "happily ever after," a narrative admission that nothing further can be said; such narratives conclude in a stylized lie, because while real lives do go on, the coherence of stories vanishes the instant the quester realizes, or fails to realize, his aim.

Housman's athlete dying young forfeits only tedious accommodations of reality, the dulling of his desire, the decline of his powers. The youthful spirit of *puer eternus* is too pure, too rarefied for the world — although, for a time, that spirit charges the world with energy, purpose, and light. But the true spirits — Goethe's young Werther, Salinger's Holden Caulfield — soon perish or break down. Dickens' plucky young protagonists seem to fare better, with a vague suggestion that they will settle down comfortably with soulmates and good positions at novel's end. But this really is narrative convenience; Pip's sentimental reunion with Estella, both of them sadder but wiser, is no more than a feebly naturalistic "happily ever after." Dickens seemed to lack the heart to follow a Pip or an Oliver through an authentic life cycle, to stay the night with Scrooge without the saving assistance of ghosts.

Mark Twain demonstrated in his boys' stories that artificial closure is superfluous. Tom Sawyer and Huck Finn neither develop nor grow up. Huck simply lights out for the western territories after his Mississippi odyssey, never to be heard from again. Herman Hesse, compulsively drawn to the difficulty of bridging youth to a meaningful life afterward, dramatized the problem directly through his male protagonists in *Narcissus and Goldmund.* Residing together in a medieval cloister, both young men are beautiful, spirited, naturally drawn to one another. Narcissus is inclined to the life of the mind: to reflection, logic, and reason. Goldmund's senses are the windows into his world. He leaves the cloister, knows many women, suffers desperate hardships, and learns to capture the fleeting way of the world in drawn and sculpted images. Toward the end of his foreshortened life Goldmund is reunited with his friend Narcissus, now a powerful abbot. Dying, Goldmund seems fully to understand his personal destiny. He feels he is being reassumed into a great cosmic mother who has indeed beckoned and haunted him all his life. Living sensually, almost instinctively, Goldmund has learned the trajectory of his life: out of earthly mother into the great cosmic mother. In dying, Goldmund achieves ultimate knowledge. But what of his cerebral friend? He asks Narcissus how he can die. The question strikes terror in Narcissus's heart.

Men die, all people die. But does the human record imply that the most fully realized male spirits die before their natural maturity is reached, or that they ought to do so? Unquestionably the record suggests that the contours of masculine youth differ dramatically from the contours of maturity. Youth is inherently heroic; age is inherently tragic. Nevertheless the mature man, the survivor, is not wholly discontinuous with his younger, questing self. To a considerable extent the younger man is contained within the older. However tempered or even weakened, the spirit of youth resonates within the old man. He can remember it and feel it in a way youth cannot possibly remember or feel maturity or old age. The mature man, however wounded or sorrowful, is more complete than the youth. It is therefore his story, not the youth's, that tells the whole masculine truth.

THREE

The Figure of David

The Lord is my shepherd; I shall not want.
—(Ps. 23:1)

*David, wearing a linen ephod, danced
without restraint before the Lord.*
—(2 Sam. 6:14)

*In iniquity I was brought to birth
and my mother conceived me in sin;
yet, though thou hast hidden the truth in darkness,
through this mystery thou dost teach me wisdom.*
—(Ps. 51:5–6)

David, son of Jesse, King and founder of united
Israel, was a fully realized man. He was a charmed and
beautiful youth, a tenacious shepherd, a fiercely spirited warrior, a wiley survivor, a lover, a poet, a visionary
king, a sinner, and a penitent. He felt himself to be

God-attached and God-directed throughout the trajectory of his long life. He attributed his triumphs and glory to God, his lapses and failures to himself. Victory and ecstasy put him in communion with the God of his fathers; betrayal and sin put him in communion with the world.

Unlike the legendary Percival, the historic David emerges into story fully potent and fully awake. He is a seventh son and faithful shepherd in the employ of his father Jesse. It is the era in which the Jews, long since returned to the promised land after their exile in Egypt, were fighting to wrest ancestral territory away from the detested Philistines. David's older brothers are away at the front; David himself is too young to enlist, although he longs to do so. As a solitary shepherd, he has contended with man-eating beasts and the elements. These things do not awe him; he is awed only by the divine Presence he experiences in the wilderness:

> The Lord is my shepherd,
> I shall not want;
> he makes me lie down in green pastures.
> He leads me beside still waters;
> he restores my soul.
> He leads me in paths of righteousness
> for his name's sake.
>
> Even though I walk through the valley of the
> shadow of death,
> I fear no evil;
> For thou art with me;

thy rod and thy staff
they comfort me.

Thou preparest a table before me in the presence
of my enemies;
thou anointest my head with oil,
my cup overflows.

Surely goodness and mercy shall follow me
all the days of my life;
and I shall dwell in the house of the Lord
for ever.

—(Ps. 23)

Unlike Percival, David does not begin his life's quest as a "little fool." He is no mama's boy; there is no mention of his mother. David's irrepressible exuberance has the appearance of naivety when, in the course of bringing provisions to his soldier brothers, he expresses his outrage at the Philistine giant, Goliath, whose daily challenge for a Hebrew champion to meet him in face-to-face combat has gone unanswered. "Who is he," David asks, "an uncircumcized Philistine, to defy the army of the living God?" (1 Sam. 17:27.) Irritated—and perhaps a little shamed—by this outburst on the part of a mere lad, David's older brother Eliab rebukes him dismissively: "I know you, you impudent young rascal; you have only come to see the fighting." (1 Sam. 17:28.)

Eliab is mistaken. David did not come merely to see the action; he is prepared to serve as an instrument of the "living God." To Saul himself, commander-in-chief of the Hebrew army, David says: "Do not lose heart, sir. I will go fight this Philistine." (1 Sam. 17:32.) David means it. As a shepherd he has killed lions and bears with his bare hands when it was necessary. With the Lord at hand, David is fearless; he is fearless throughout his life. Again unlike Percival, David is not obsessed by the form and trappings of a warrior. He does not long for uniform, weaponry, or armor. In fact, when Saul offers the boy his own tunic and helmet and coat of mail, David declines them: "I cannot go with these, because I have not tried them" (1 Sam. 17:39).

With his stick, a sling, and a handful of smooth pebbles from a brook, David goes forth to fight the strongest man in the world. Like Percival's Red Knight, Goliath is arrogantly abusive of the young rustic who has come to challenge him, and like the Red Knight, Goliath is quickly dispatched. A single slung stone knocked the giant senseless, and with Goliath's own sword David beheaded him, causing the Philistine army to flee in terror.

King Saul was so taken with the young hero that he took him into his household, where he immediately became a beloved soul-mate of Saul's son Jonathan. Jonathan's allegiance to David, where suspicion and jealousy might have been expected, was pledged in a mutual compact "because each loved the other as dearly as himself" (1 Sam. 18:3). To express the extent of his commitment, Jonathan gave David his tunic, sword, bow, and belt. Earlier David had declined to accept Saul's costume and arms. They were strange to him, and he could not rely on them in a mortal crisis. Jonathan's gift is love itself, and David instinctively trusts it.

Saul bestows upon David both a place in the royal household and a military command, but David's fame and favor are even greater among the masses. "Saul made havoc among thousands but David among tens of thousands," they chant (1 Sam. 18:7). David is aligned with God's will, and the people are aligned with David. He is invincible, but not unassailable. Saul is soon jealous of David, and the jealousy will fester into hatred.

But as Saul's lieutenant, as the young giant-killer, the scourge of the Philistines, David is jubilant. An instrument of the living God, he fears no man, can do no wrong. Here he has reached a distinctive masculine pitch: God's favor has not made him safe, has not given him peace; it has vaulted him beyond any concern for his safety, even for his very life. David has a mission and experiences the deep love of male fellowship. These are the components of warrior ecstasy. Next to these, mortal safety counts for nothing. Although increasingly "politically incorrect" in the aftermath of this century's world wars, warrior ecstasy has found a voice throughout the history of civilization. Shakespeare's Henry V is especially compelling on this theme. On the eve of St. Crispian, about to go, woefully outnumbered, into battle against the French at Agincourt, Henry exhorts his fellows:

This story shall the good man teach his son;
. . . From this day to the ending of the world,
but we in it shall be remembered;
we few, we happy few, we band of brothers;
For he today that sheds his blood with me
Shall be my brother; be he ne'er so vile,

This day shall gentle his condition:
And gentlemen in England now a-bed
Shall think themselves accursed they were
    not here,
And hold their manhoods cheap whiles any
    speaks
That fought with us on St. Crispin's day.

—Henry V, IV, iv.

There is a Freudian habit of mind that insists on seeing male forcefulness, whether martial or athletic, as a compensation for an inability to love, for failed intimacy. Neither the historical nor the literary record can be made to support such a position, except by willful distortion. The tendency to see purposeful combat as a mistake, a mistake which can be corrected by emotional intimacy, was seen clearly in the anti-Viet Nam war sentiment of the 1960s, specifically in its ideological slogan-formula: "Make love, not war." A good example of the era's polarization of lovemaking and war-making was revealed in the 1979 anti-war film, *Coming Home*, in which an army officer incapable of sexual or other intimacy is cuckolded by a paraplegic veteran who has come to reject war. The pacifist-cripple is portrayed—vividly—as one who can sexually gratify the active soldier's wife; the film concludes as the soldier-husband strips himself naked on a deserted beach, then swims out into the surf, presumably to his death.

The figure of David stands in sharp opposition to the late twentieth century notion that forcefulness and intimacy are incompatible. At the height of his fame and effectiveness as a fighter, the young David achieved a deep intimacy with both Jonathan and, later, Jonathan's sister Michal. Homoerotic relations were considered an abomination in Hebrew scripture, and perhaps to some extent because of this, the depth of affection between David and Jonathan could be professed without shame:

So Jonathan and David made a solemn compact because each loved the other as dearly as himself.

David is gentle and loving. David is also a warrior-prince. The pleasing tension between these qualities is captured astonishingly in the contrasting figures of David cast by the Florentine masters Donatello and Michelangelo. Donatello's David is preadolescent, girlishly effeminate. There are silky expanses of skin, but no defined muscles. He rests on a sword so long and heavy that he could not imaginably wield it. He stands naked, but not robustly naked in the Hellenistic manner; he is rather demure, his eyes downcast. Apart from the sword, the only other martial signature is the pair of military boots he wears, but even these are stylishly cut and dainty. On his head, where one might reasonably expect a helmet, there is something like a broad bonnet, wreathed in flowers. Altogether, this is a surprising figure to be standing with one foot poised saucily on Goliath's great severed head. Michelangelo's David is, by contrast, physically potent. He is a young man, but he is powerfully muscled. His bearing is regal and his gaze is straight ahead; he fears nothing. While comfortably at rest, Michelangelo's figure is at the same time poised for action. The powerful right arm and the slightly curled hand are more than up to the task of slinging lethal stones into a giant's skull. Donatello's David stands five feet two and a half inches; Michelangelo's is thirteen feet five inches. Both hauntingly evoke the biblical David.

David's love of women—Michal, Bathsheba—is preceded by his deep love for his friend and soul-mate, Jonathan. This depth of feeling, hovering somewhere between the amorous and the friendly, is itself a common feature of boys' and men's stories since antiquity. Pairs of Arthurian knights quested together in this spirit. Pip and Herbert Pocket of *Great Expectations*, David Copperfield and Steerforth, Tom Brown and East in *Tom Brown's Schooldays*, Phineas and Gene in *A Separate Peace*, Tom Sawyer and Huckleberry Finn, and, again, Hesse's Narcissus and Goldmund—these committed, loving friendships fortify a male's development in a distinctive and possibly necessary way. Charles Ryder, Evelyn Waugh's melancholy protagonist in *Brideshead Revisited*, sees his boyhood lover-friend, Sebastian Flyte, as a "forerunner" in a romantic unfolding that comes to full expression in his love for Sebastian's sister, Julia.

David is a lover, a lover of men and a lover of women. He deeply loves and respects his elders, and his love for his own children is inexhaustible. Moreover, his depth as a lover is never opposed to his strength as a warrior. In David, love and force are not antithetical. Even when he is gentlest and most patient, David is potent and, one might argue, potentially dangerous. Gentleness in males may lie in a conscious and loving restraint of force. Robert Bly points out that Odysseus had occasion periodically to "show his sword," but not to use it.[18] Similarly, David reveals his greatest strength when he intentionally forgoes an aggressive action of which he is fully capable. He is not gentle because he is timid or weak; his strength enables him to be gentle, to choose it.

At the point in his early career when he became more popular and more beloved among the people of Israel than King Saul himself, David falls out of favor with the king. Furious and jealous, Saul loses his sanity when he hears the popular chant:

> Saul made havoc among thousands,
> but David among tens of thousands.

Without explaining it to David or ever fully understanding it himself, Saul makes David his mortal enemy, attempting several times to kill him and forcing him to flee the royal court and to set up as an outlaw in the contested territories occupied by the Philistines. With only the sword of the slain Goliath to defend himself, David endures an undeserved exile, a test which deepens him. Twice during his exile, David is given an opportunity in which he could have captured or killed Saul. The first of these occurred when the king and 3,000 retainers had set out to destroy David and a small band of his fellow outlaws in the wilderness. In the course of this mission, Saul stops to relieve himself in the very cave where David and his men are hiding. Recognizing the King, David's mates urge him to seize Saul. This David vehemently refuses to do, although he does sneak up close enough to where Saul is resting to cut off a snippet of his cloak. David quietly followed Saul out of the cave before he hailed him:

> My Lord the King ... Why do you listen when they say that David is out to do you harm? Today you can see for yourself that the Lord put you into my power in the cave; I had a mind to kill you, but no, I spared your life and said, "I cannot lift a finger against my master, for he is the Lord's anointed." Look, my dear lord, look at this piece of your cloak in my hand. I cut it off, but I did not kill you; this will show that I have no thought of violence or treachery against you, and that I have done you no wrong; yet you are resolved to take my life.
>
> —1 Sam. 24:10–12

Later, when Saul and his sons, including Jonathan, are killed in the course of fighting the Philistines, David grieves deeply. He grieves for his persecutor Saul—"delightful and dearly loved"—and for his soul mate, Jonathan:

> I grieve for you, Jonathan my brother; dear and delightful you were to me; your love for me was wonderful, surpassing the love of women.
>
> —2 Sam. 1:26

When he is thirty years old, David is anointed king
by the elders of Israel. Already wise and durable and
deep, he will reign for forty years. As king, he will rid
Israel of its most longstanding enemies. He will found a
capitol fortress-city on a hill: Jerusalem. He will create a
national army, undertake a massive program of public
works. He will codify the laws and establish a judicial
system to apply them. Having recovered the Ark of the
Covenant, David rededicates the people of Israel to the
worship of the god of their fathers.

As a boy and a young man, David was the hero of
his tribe; as a man, he is the king of a civil state. As a
hero, he was spirited, intuitive; as head of state, he is
discerning. David emerges from a state of nature into
the conventions of politics, from unconscious virtue to
the conscious stewardship of the public good. In Greek
political theory, the passage from personal concerns
into public ones is the ultimate human achievement,
the passage from tribal life to civic life the ultimate
social achievement. A vision of the human city, and of
justice within the city, is not given to everybody; it is
limited to a disciplined and discerning few—heroes
tempered by wisdom and experience: philosophers.

David negotiates this passage from the personal to
the public, from unconsciousness to consciousness,
from shepherd to king, boy to man. His trajectory is, he
feels, God-infused from the beginning. He is an instrument of God, a servant, not a power unto himself. At
the height of his power, David confesses to God:

Thou hast made good thy word; it was thy
purpose to spread thy servant's fame, and so

thou has raised me to this greatness. Great
indeed art thou, O Lord God; we have never
heard of one like thee; there is no god but
thee.

—2 Sam. 7:21–23

And then, for no apparent reason (although every
man understands it perfectly), David falls. He indulges
a passionate interest in a beautiful woman, Bathsheba,
whom he observes while she is bathing. As king he
knows he can summon her to his court, and he does so,
seducing her despite his knowledge that she is the wife
of one of his loyal soldiers, Uriah the Hittite. Every
possible law, convention, and propriety is violated. The
Hebrews of that era permitted polygamy, but strictly
forbade adultery. Moreover, David had intercourse
with Bathsheba during her post-menstrual purification,
a time traditionally set aside for abstinence. As it happened, Bathsheba became pregnant and let David
know it.

Embarrassed and afraid for his reputation, David
sinks more deeply into deception and crime. He calls
Uriah back from active duty, in the hope that he will
sleep with his wife and assume the paternity of the
child to be born. But Uriah, true to the soldier's custom
of his day, has vowed to foreswear intercourse while
actively campaigning. David tries to soften Uriah's resolve by making him drunk. Still Uriah does not go to
his wife's bed. Now desperate, David hatches a plan to
have Uriah killed. He orders him back to the front and
sends secret instructions to his general Joab to assign

Uriah to fierce combat and then, by prearrangement, to order his fellow soldiers to fall back. This plan was executed, Uriah duly killed. Afterward, David brought Bathsheba into his household and married her.

There is nothing generous or public-spirited in any of this on David's part. He cannot even be said to be heroically impulsive. He violates laws and customs that he himself endorses. He wilfully betrays his own standards. He is also shrewd about it. Nevertheless, his crime comes to light. A courageous holy man seeks David out:

> The Lord sent Nathan the Prophet to David, and when he entered his presence, he said to him, 'There were once two men in the same city, one rich and the other poor. The rich man had large flocks and herds, but the poor man had nothing of his own except one little ewe lamb. He reared it himself, and it grew up in his home with his own sons. It ate from his dish, drank from his cup and nestled in his arms; it was like a daughter to him. One day a traveler came to the rich man's house, and he, too mean to take something from his own flocks and herds to serve up to his guest, took the poor man's lamb and served up that.'
>
> David was very angry, and burst out, 'As the Lord lives, the man who did this deserves to die! He shall pay for the lamb four times over, because he has done this thing and

shown no pity.' Then Nathan said to David,
'You are the man . . .'

—2 Sam. 12:1–6

David of course was the man, a sinner. In this he
realized he was no longer God's agent, God's servant;
he was no longer charmed. At this emotional juncture,
he could have completed his break with the God-con-
nected righteousness he had always felt to be part of
his nature; he could have put away Nathan, killed him.
He could have defied God or social conventions, even
elevating his defiance to a political principle: for who
should impede the will of a great king? David could
have liberated himself by declaring himself the sole
arbiter of right and wrong, the custodian of his own
soul. He could have in this way been a thoroughly
modern man. Instead, David submits to Nathan's chas-
tisement: "I have sinned against the Lord."

From this point forward, as if in retribution,
David's life becomes as strife-ridden and burdensome
as his youthful career had been favored by fortune. He
endures civil war and the insurrection of a beloved son,
Absalom. In duress, David's story loses the aura of
legend and assumes historicity. But even in weariness,
deepest grief, and the humiliating infirmities of old
age, David retains a greatness. While a fallen man, one
who has consciously forfeited grace for the allures of
the world, David nonetheless knows the difference; he
has sinned against God, but he has not denied Him. He
has violated his own nature, but he has not renounced
it. He is not Lear, not Mr. Kurtz.

In decline, David lost grace, but he did not lose what he had learned of grace. A great man, ultimately a great sinner, David knew better. Moreover, he stood by what he knew. From his deathbed he tells Solomon, his son and heir:

> Be strong and show yourself a man. Fulfill your duty to the Lord your God.
>
> — 1 Kings 2:1

The masculine trajectory is up and away. It is an ascent, and as David's story suggests, it is an ascent Godward. As Erikson noted of small boys at play, ascent is often succeeded by a fall: towers topple to ruins. But ruins are not the end of it. Out of the ruins, the male spirit may stir, may rise — inspiringly — again. This from David the psalmist:

> Create a pure heart in me, O God, and give me a new and steadfast spirit; do not drive me from thy presence or take thy holy spirit from me; revive in me the joy of thy deliverance and grant me a willing spirit to uphold me. I will teach transgressors the ways that lead to thee, and sinners shall return to thee again.
>
> — Ps. 51:1–4

FOUR

Actual Boys: A Personal Perspective

Smart lad, to slip betimes away
From fields where glory does not stay
And early though the laurel grows
It withers quicker than the rose.
And round that early-laurelled head
Will flock to gaze the strengthless dead
And find unwithered on its curls
The garland briefer than a girl's.

A.E. Housman,
To An Athlete Dying Young

When I was twenty-three years old, I took a job teaching in a boys' college preparatory school. At the time it seemed an expedient, and probably temporary, thing to do. I had been a graduate student, I had no money, and I was engaged to be married. The school, as I assessed it, was solid enough; its all-boys composition did not figure much into my deliberations.

51

I had known graduates of such schools in college: "prep school" boys who, despite clear individual differences, seemed also, in some way I had not bothered to define, to bear a common stamp. If I had examined that impression further, I suppose I would have concluded that this boys' school "mark" derived from wealth and class, also perhaps from the experience of living together in a kind of spartan intimacy. When my prep school friends talked about their school lives, there was a depth of feeling that was foreign to me. Some of them were affectionately wistful about alma mater, and some seemed strangely dependent on former friends and faculty. Many were openly hostile to the schools they had left, resentful of remembered restrictions, bruised by discipline or low appraisals of their abilities.

As a graduate of midwestern public schools, I shared no such feelings. My schooling had been coeducational from kindergarten onward. School life seemed a seamless continuation of life in the town where I lived. The school buildings were solidly made, brightly lit, spacious, and clean. The faculty, until junior high school nearly all of them women, were on balance competent and professional. Although more than half of the graduates of my high school went on to college, I recall no one who felt especially engaged or inspired or intellectually directed by the school. The high school was large—more than twice the size of the liberal arts college I attended—and of necessity highly routinized and, I suppose, a little impersonal. The social agenda of my "set"—both friendships and amorous arrangements—seemed to me infinitely engaging, seemed actually to provide the energy and the emotional substance of the school enterprise. It would never have dawned on me to call my schooling "good" or "important."

By contrast, my undergraduate experience, while hardly distinguished by disciplined achievement on my part, was intellectually thrilling. Teachers seemed eccentric, hard-edged, personable, many of them brilliant. Great cultural figures—Plato, Machiavelli, Keats—came vividly alive through the explication of their work. But returning to a school, a boys' prep school, to teach—I really did not know what I could fairly expect.

My first and most vivid impression was of how thoroughly male a boys' school felt. The presence of so many boys and men was not at all repellent. The absence of girls and the scarcity of women was harder to get used to, especially at first. I remember being fascinated by how much the relative absence of females intensified my awareness of the few who did pass through my perceptual field in the course of the school day: an elderly librarian, the office receptionist, the art teacher, some older boy's girlfriend on the football sidelines. This was no simple erotic arousal; it was a heightened awareness of the otherness, of seemingly every feature of these women and girls. I believe this period of my life advanced me a long way toward seeing and appreciating the astonishing individuality and range of females.

The converse did not occur: the immersion in maleness did not blur or generalize the features of the boys. From the outset, their individuality surfaced in clear, often eccentric relief. As one who had grown up, I had always assumed, a "boy's boy"—from earliest memory moving in packs, then cliques of male friends, crazy about sports, susceptible to the inspiration of questers, swashbucklers, and romantic heroes—I was surprised by much of what I saw in my new school. There were instinctively gracious and even beautifully mannered boys (as well as plenty of noble savages), but there were no "regular," "average," what used to be called "all-American" boys. No one seemed to me merely well-rounded. Their talents, introversions, extroversions, even their occasional pathologies were vividly realized. To me at twenty-three and newly married, they seemed surprisingly far along in the realization of what was distinctive about them. They seemed older and bolder than my boyhood friends in the things they would risk saying or taking on. They also seemed younger in their absence of inhibition; the toughest and most worldly-wise among them seemed to me more vulnerable than the warier and thus blander companions of my schooldays.

This was of course a college preparatory school, and most of the boys threw themselves into their school work with an almost worrying lack of perspective. From the outset, my students accomplished things beyond my highest expectations, often failing, and failing devastatingly, to realize their own. Working among them, I found it impossible to maintain my own detachment, "adult" perspective, critical distance. I remember struggling to find words to describe the school climate to my wife and being able only to come up with: "There's such an edge to the place." It was a stimulating edge. To my surprise, I found that for the first time in my life I was wholly engaged in the task before me: on a kind of train with no clear plan or desire to get off.

To some extent, every new teacher begins his or her work as something of an impostor. Before we can really do it—introduce, clarify points of knowledge; devise activities that exercise students in such a way that they will master them—we play at teaching, strike teacherly poses, hope we are credible. The younger the teacher, the more effortful the debut. Perhaps a carefully designed system of teacher-training in which a master teacher initiates an apprentice is the best way to launch a young teacher, but that was not possible in my school; the other teachers were too heavily loaded with responsibilities to ease me through my initiation.

It was a kind of initiation, and even now, after twenty-five years in the classroom, teaching boys still feels a little like initiation. On balance, I believe this has been very good for me. Any progress I have made in the direction of authenticity in my teaching and my other communications with students has been elicited by the boys' own extraordinary authenticity. And that lesson is continuing. However one assesses its emotional charge or moral value, the social climate of boys together is radically authentic. There is not of course a "type" of boy; there are types.

The dramatic realization of these several types tends to confirm and to celebrate a corporate sense of maleness in the community generally. Such communities feel especially alive. Distinctive boys remind every boy of who he is.

FUNNY BOYS

School is so serious. The training for adult work—
for maturity itself—is even more so. Moreover, there is
no drama in life, and thus no life worth having, unless
it is serious. From a developing boy's perspective, the
stakes really are high. You can win or lose big, make it
or not make it at all. Exercising the ability a boy actually has—executing a surprising, tight run on the guitar; extending arms, hands, fingertips to pull in the
miraculous pass in the end zone—can, in the right
circumstances, vault him into unimaginable celebrity
and happiness. The feats of enduring boys' stories
come true every day of the week. It is also in every
boy's range, not just bad ones, to decide (or to fail to
decide) to try something that will result in colossal
failure or trouble. Mistakes, terrible decisions, repellent
behaviors occur so fast they hardly seem deliberate at
all. A boy feels more witness to, than an agent of, his
own delinquency: the stone already through the window, the punch thrown, drunk or high before he knew
it, the tape deck pinched, pants down, the answer
copied, the deadly vehicle already into the intersection.
Every boy is closer to crime, closer to the big mistake
than we can comfortably acknowledge.

Boys together cannot help composing a drama in
which it is right to strive and to be good and to succeed,
but the odds are sickeningly against it. School is so
serious. And because school is so serious, humor is
salvation: not polite humor, not the clichés, the posturings, derived from television programs and other commercial culture—but the instinctive, spontaneous,

sometimes anarchic impulse to deny the seriousness of everything, to set up an alternative system in which the preposterous reigns.

The seriousness of the Middle Ages was mitigated by periodic Feasts of Fools. They were not polite. They were outrageous: bishops, magistrates, sacred rites, decorum, sexual propriety, sobriety — all were lampooned and usurped in an exhilarating, if temporary, festival. Feasts of Fools were initiated by males for reasons that still pertain.

The fall of my first year, even before I could confidently find my way around my school's warren of classrooms and corridors, I became aware that something unsettling was in the air. Some senior boys had formed a dubious arts-related society and had managed to legitimize themselves to the extent of getting a rather vague older teacher to serve as its advisor — the tacit understanding being that neither the society nor the advisor would bother one another. What was this society? I recall that it bore a formal name — say, the Ernest M. Babbitt Society. I cannot remember all of the charter members, but three or four ringleaders were unforgettable. There was a very tall, bespectacled boy whose smile was so broad and so unvarying that he seemed alternately simple-minded and supercilious. He was a poor student, cheerfully behind in all his assignments, ingenuously apologetic, thoroughly unreliable. His classmates loved him, laughing with and at him in equal measure. If there was a leader to the new, and as it happened short-lived, society, it was a wiry, blade-faced boy who wore his longish hair glossily lubricated, parted in the center, and swept back in a way that made him, in photographs, look like a schoolboy at the turn of the century. He rarely smiled. Very bright, rapid of speech, he presented a wide-eyed, mock seriousness when he spoke to teachers or when he had an occasion to make some kind of announcement to the school. A third member looked a bit like Huck Finn gone unhappy. Wildly unkempt, he too was scholastically advanced, but he seemed paler, less engaged, less happy than his friends. A fourth member stands out only for his irrepressible silliness. Seemingly always either talking or laughing, he was himself a comical-looking figure with black hair and brows, black glasses and a nose so prominent that he almost looked as though he were wearing one of those glasses-false nose assemblies that make the wearer look a little like Groucho Marx. This boy seemed always to be in a state of high hilarity about what the society members were up to. But in truth, no one was sure what the society was up to. They met frequently, in and out of school. They kept each other's company almost exclusively. At first suspiciously, then demonstrably, the senior faculty came to dislike and finally to oppose them.

The society's first gesture that made any sort of impact on the school was the publication of an eccentric paper called "The Voice of Cheese." This appeared fairly randomly and consisted of three or four pages of mimeographed typescript interspersed with puzzling illustrations. "The Voice of Cheese" was not duplicated and distributed among the students; instead its pages were tacked neatly onto a student bulletin board in the locker area. For some reason, everybody in the school, including faculty, seemed to read it. The wonder of it

was that the surreal drift of the articles made no out-
ward sense whatsoever, except perhaps to the members of the society whose in-jokes and private irrever-
ences were no doubt encoded in the text.

A conviction that the authors of the "Voice of
Cheese" were "up to something," and that it was not
good, soon took hold among the faculty; the students
were too interested in it, thought it was too funny. At
length, one of the paper's features, a serial titled, I
believe, "The Adventures of Ronnie the Raven," was
said to be making derogatory references to the school's
football coach, a small, volatile man, and to his wife,
who worked in the student book store. I recall reading
the questionable columns, and while I could tell that
certain things the coach and his wife had said or done
did come obliquely into play, the references were so
glancing and were embedded in so nonsensical a vehicle that it was hard to imagine finding them offensive.
The coach, however, felt otherwise. The very possibility of his being made a figure of fun enraged him,
and not being able to follow the drift of "The Voice of
Cheese" made things worse. One morning I saw him
make his way through a cluster of boys at the bulletin
board. As he stood squinting at a newly mounted edition of "The Voice of Cheese," the boys fell silent.
Then the coach ripped the pages from the board,
crumpled them into a ball, and strode away with them.

With this striking gesture, "The Voice of Cheese"
ceased publication, although the blade-faced editor
persisted for days questioning, with elaborate courtesy,
the coach's motives. The "Cheese" staffers animatedly
asked their friends and any teachers who could be

made to listen why the coach had acted so aggressively. There were letters to the editor of the (official) school newspaper. "What has happened to 'The Cheese'?" "What did Ronnie the Raven do wrong?" There seemed to be no serious way to address—or to re-dress—any of this. For no obvious reason, the appearance of the paper had made the boys laugh. Faculty suspicious about the paper's meaning made the boys laugh. Ripping the paper from the bulletin board made the boys laugh, as did mock-protesting such a gesture.

Later that year, when I had gotten to know fairly well the boys who organized the society, I asked if they would help me celebrate my 24th birthday party by serving as waiters. I lived in a rural stable building, in an apartment above a decrepit garage. It was a small, extremely modest party, and I had no need whatsoever of hired help, but I thought it would be, for that very reason, amusing to present an appearance of "staff" to my friends. With only the most cursory instructions—"would you guys mind coming to my party and pretending to be waiters?"—the "Voice of Cheese" boys outdid themselves.

When a noisy crowd of well-wishers had gathered in my cramped rooms, the gangling figures of the boys suddenly appeared. They wore tuxedos, and their hair was slicked back preposterously. Serious of demeanor, each bore a tray of what looked at first glance like canapés. On closer examination, the offerings were very peculiar: a McDonald's cheeseburger cut into perhaps twenty tiny sections; small, withered raisins pierced by toothpicks; free-standing little dollups of mayonnaise; crudely made sandwich halves with large bites obviously taken out of them; bits of doughnut;

Q-tips, nail scissors, an old tweezers; little packets of postage stamps. Before each item was a neatly printed cardboard price tag, and the prices were phenomenally high—the cheeseburger fragments $11.50, the nail scissors $9.00.

The boys responded to all questions, expressions of surprise, and (at first guarded) laughter with deadpan, matter-of-fact courtesy: "Yes, that is the price, $11.50. It's an actual part of a cheeseburger from McDonald's, and we are offering it to you for sale this evening." My friends looked to me for some explanation, some clue, and I remember deciding not to provide any. I purchased a few items, and so did some of my guests. When they had made their impact as waiters, but before anyone could have been said to have gotten "used to" them, the boys put down their trays, assembled themselves in the middle of the sitting room, and called for the guests' attention. "Because this is a birthday party," the blade-faced boy said, "we would like to sing." They sang "Mother" (" 'M' is for the million things she gave me, 'O' means only that she's growing old . . ."), contorting their bodies to form each letter. They followed the songs with what they called "hand skits": mock magic tricks in which, for instance, a fist with one finger extended would be transformed, by being smacked by the boy's other fist, into a fist with two fingers extended. The hand skits were performed wordlessly and with intense gravity, the non-performing boys humming "Fine and Dandy" in the background, breaking to a loud "Ta-dah!" at trick's end. They did a few of these, accepted raucous applause, then hurried down the stairs out of the apartment.

I followed them down into the garage and

thanked them warmly for coming. "Our pleasure," said the blade-faced boy. Then they rummaged through their pockets and, against my objections, returned the money my friends and I had given them for the items on the trays. It amounted to a surprisingly large sum.

Being funny is a gift, and the boys who have it are transformed beatifically. Moreover, boys together have a quick, intuitive sense of what is really funny, and when it appears, they erupt, they roar. Boys appreciate genuinely odd people, not the practiced wise-guy. Being funny is a revered gift; trying to be funny is loathsome. I recall a former student whose funniness made a sustained and healing impact on the school for several years running.

* * *

His given name was Tom, but he performed under the stage name, Professor Fate. Emphatically unathletic and overweight, he had some of the owlish madness of the actors Zero Mostel and Robert Morley. He was no clown, however. He was a magician, professional enough that he charged fees when he performed at children's parties. In performance — say, in a school variety show — he was deeply earnest and ploddingly methodical. I cannot remember any humorous lines in his routines. Yet the mere mention of the name Professor Fate sent the assembled school into hilarity. The first glimpse of him on stage in his magician's top hat and tails would elicit a bedlam of pleasure.

He was a terrible magician. This was not simply because his tricks did not come off (as was frequently

the case), but more because of the resigned, slightly
melancholy air he conveyed throughout his routine.
Like certain vaudeville comics, he had, though in his
case unintentionally, the ability to forecast that nothing entertaining would transpire—certainly nothing
magical—in the minutes ahead. His tux was ill-fitting,
dusty, bagged at the knees. His demonstration stand
and assorted apparatus also looked as if they had been
knocked about considerably. Wires tended to show.
Silk scarves knotted together were easily observable
behind his lapel. His torso and sleeves bulged unnatu-
rally with ill-concealed objects: eggs, coins, cards,
stuffed rabbits, feather dusters.

My own favorite moment in any Professor Fate
performance came when he would announce that it
was time for "close-in magic." By this he meant that he
would be working with small objects: peas concealed
under little bowls, cards, match sticks. In a close, intimate setting such as a birthday child's family room,
these "close-in" tricks might conceivably engage attention. But on stage in a large assembly hall, even those
seated in the first and second rows could not really see
what was going on in one of Professor Fate's "close-in"
tricks. In any event, Professor Fate's sleight-of-hand
was hardly a professional strength. Invariably the volunteers who came on stage to "pick a card, any card" or
to guess how many peas were under each bowl would
foil the trick by guessing correctly or denying that the
card the professor produced (after much hesitant shuf-
fling and deck tapping) was the one originally selected.
By the time this had happened, the audience's pitch of
hilarity was acute, but it would somehow intensify

when Professor Fate would half-heartedly challenge the volunteer: "Are you sure you picked the queen of clubs?" "Are you absolutely sure that's what you want your guess to be—three peas under this bowl?" The volunteers always stuck to their guns, and Professor Fate would look after them pensively as they returned to their seats.

For me, and I believe for many, the comic force of this "close-in" sequence did not derive from any ineptitude or failure of execution. The humor lay in the fact that no one except Professor Fate himself could really see what he was doing. His pudgy hands obscuring the little red bowls as he slid them over some quantity of alleged peas, he would narrate developments as best he could: "And so—just when you might expect to find all three peas under bowl number two, we lift it up to find—oh, wait a minute . . ." Long spells would pass in silence as he puzzled over the elusive technicalities of the trick.

Once the boys in a middle-school assembly were genuinely unkind to Professor Fate. Knowing in advance that he was to appear, they made a crude plan to harass him, even to throw things at him on stage. Several times during the routine, he was showered with shiny little metallic objects, mainly paper clips. Then and then only did I hear Professor Fate complain. Afterward, when the boys were scolded and the ringleaders sent home, several of us tried our best to console him. "I wasn't that bad this afternoon," he said. "I wasn't that bad." To our righteously angry words about the boys who had thrown things onto the stage, he said, "I didn't mind the paper clips. What can they do? But I minded the pins. There were a few pins, and they really sting you."

Over the course of some hard to chart stretch between his tenth- and eleventh-grade year, Tom grew out of his Professor Fate persona and into, I suppose, himself. Now a lanky, physically comfortable man in his thirties, he has dedicated himself to making documentary films about the deaf. He seems almost to emanate kindness and patience. The easy smile is new. Only in his eyes can one detect a faint trace of Professor Fate: something owlish, something both merry and wary.

* * *

I am inexpressibly grateful for funny boys. Without them the work I love would be, literally, unendurable. The humor of boys together punctuates the annual school cycle as if according to some loony grand plan. I cannot pass the classroom I was first assigned to teach in without recalling Mike, an eighth grader with hair like Brillo pads, whose standard greeting was to slide to his knees, fling his arms out wide, shake his head in a palsied manner, and exclaim with unbounded pleasure, "It's me!" Nor does much time pass without a vivid memory of a sweet-natured boy named Ace, who once, while helping me to paint my classroom, confided that he could sometimes pull in AM radio through his braces directly into his head—but only Detroit. Again, very few funny boys are jokers. At the wretched low point of his parents' divorce, one of my most taciturn students, Steve Benton, was able to send himself into fits of laughter by signing his name Steve "Steve" Benton. School is so serious.

HELPLESS BOYS

Boys misbehave. They are capable of breathtaking regressions and lapses. Steeling himself to call up a girl he has recently met, an otherwise presentable teenager will dial the number, hear her father say hello, and slam down the phone in a panic. A reflexively mannerly student of mine once lost his composure in the course of being upbraided by the school dean and said, "Excuse me, sir, but aren't you being kind of an asshole?" Before he knew it, the words were out. Before they know it, boys misbehave.

I was the dean myself when I was called on to respond to the worst fight ever to come to my attention at school. Though only seconds in duration, the violence was electric and, I am told by eye-witnesses, terrifying to watch. The guilty party, the aggressor, was a senior boy named Len whom I liked, and still like, very much. Darren, the victim, was a boy it was then impossible to like.

The fight, it turned out, had been brewing for weeks. The antipathy began when Len, in the course of serving on the Student Discipline Committee, of which he was an elected member, issued the first of what would be several disciplinary measures against Darren, a sophomore. Darren's offenses were not grave, but they were relentless: cutting classes, forging notes and signatures, inscribing repellent graffiti on desks and locker faces. From a faculty perspective, Darren presented a provocatively ornery facade. In class he was unprepared, undisclosing, occasionally defiant. If circumstances allowed, he would bait weaker, unpopular students under his breath. To teachers who would tolerate it, he was sarcastic, dismissive of the material under review. Outside of class, he was energized by teasing campaigns against various perceived enemies. In these he could be very effective, even vicious. Like many bright, fundamentally unhappy boys, Darren had an acute intuitive sense of what could hurt another person. Inevitably, perhaps, he launched a campaign of abuse against Len.

It is possible that he simply misread or underestimated Len's volatility, although I suspect that Darren may have read him perfectly. Len, while a focal senior, a civic booster, and a jock, was on a number of counts hypersensitive and therefore vulnerable. His family was not well-off, and he was anxious about what he believed was their lack of sophistication. Generally, Len was hungrier for approval than a typical underclassman might have thought. An earnest, hardworking student-athlete, he did not suffer much gratuitous kidding or abuse, but what came his way bothered him. He was especially concerned that his neighborhood friends, whom he had "forsaken" to attend a private school, not think ill of him. In this regard, he had to walk a difficult line. With his old friends he did not want to appear snobbish or too intellectual or in any way altered by the "preppy" world. Nor did he want to give the impression that he hadn't been successful, hadn't "made it" in the world of his new school.

In other words, accomplishments and status aside, Len was as vulnerable as any teenage boy, and Darren somehow knew it. He began taunting Len shortly after Darren's first "conviction" by the Discipline Committee. In the hearing itself, and then afterwards, he referred to Len sarcastically as "sir." He was able to parlay this ploy into classroom-wide laughter when Len, one of whose scholarship jobs was to take classroom attendance, would make his daily stop in Darren's English class. When Len looked into the room to get the teacher's attendance count, Darren would exclaim with mock enthusiasm, "Oh, look — it's sir!" or "We're all here today, sir!" Len took the bait, reddened, was inarticulately furious.

At one point, after graffiti and anonymous messages had exacerbated the "sir" business, Len sought out the faculty Discipline Committee advisor to complain that Darren and his friends were a bunch of really rotten kids who were up to no good. The advisor heard Len out and inquired after specifics, but Len provided none. He was not a boy who would "narc" on another student, especially for anonymous graffiti, the very appearance of which, had he been able to admit it, made him feel unbearably ashamed.

One winter afternoon, Darren escalated the tension to a dangerous pitch. He accompanied some friends to a basketball game against Len's previous high school. Noticing Darren's school jacket, some of Len's neighborhood friends who attended the high school asked Darren if he knew Len. And how was he doing anyway? Darren saw a welcome opening. He told the boys that Len was one of the most "pitiful" people in the school, "a joke," a "pseudo-jock" no one took seriously: in the parlance of the day, "a dweeb." Because Darren's friends laughed as this account was being rendered, Len's neighborhood friends may have believed this was actually his status at school. In any event, the appraisal, including the derogatory labels, were conveyed to Len that evening. The insults were deeply felt. Moreover, because there was a weekend's time to think about them, Len seemed, to those who noticed, to be in an almost altered state when he came to school on Monday morning. As reported by his friends later, he did not respond to any of the usual before-school conversational banter; he sat with eyes glazed through the morning assembly. The only words anyone can remember Len uttering before the incident itself were: "Where is he? I'm going to kill him." One boy heard sufficient tension in Len's voice that he pressed him about what was wrong. "I've just had enough," Len said. "I'm going to kill that kid."

When the bell sounded for the daily mid-morning break, Len set out to find Darren. One of Len's best friends, and the closest witness to the "fight," reported seeing Len standing motionless in the center of the student commons, his eyes fixed on Darren as he chatted with another student. Again sensing the tension, Len's friend asked him what was wrong. Len did not answer but continued staring at Darren. Then Darren turned away from his companion, met Len's eyes and said, "What's your problem?"

Without running, but seeming to cover the ground between them in an instant, Len crossed the commons, grabbed a handful of Darren's sweater, and pulled him up close. "Did you call me a 'dweeb'?" Len did not wait for an answer. The affected look of contempt on Darren's face ignited the vast inner dread of contempt that had been building since Len had heard the first supercilious "sir."

Len then drove his fist ringingly and brutally into the side of Darren's face. The force of the blow snapped the frame of Darren's glasses and drove a broken edge into his cheek, creating a gash. Beneath the skin, it was later discovered, there was more serious injury: a cheek bone, including the orbit around his right eye, was fractured. The friend was able to wrestle Len apart from Darren before he could hit him again, which was clearly the intention.

The student commons was at once charged with tension. A cadre of faculty swarmed to the scene, some tending to the gashed and blinking Darren, who now lay prostrate on the floor, others to Len and his friend.

A minute or two later, a colleague who, as it happened, was unaware of the fracture in Darren's skull, brought him to my office. Snuffling, sputtering, and daubing his cut with tissue, Darren made his way across my office to the small couch and lay down.

"What happened, Darren?" I asked.

"Len just beat the shit out of me," he said with surprising force. There was nothing accusatory in his tone, nor any trace of complaint. There was, rather, excitement in his voice, as though he had discovered something vivid and important. I remember feeling, even writing down, "Darren seemed oddly elated by his assault." Although he managed to give me a coherent account of the blow, even some of the background business that led to it, Darren came back several times to his original revelation. "He beat the shit out of me. He just beat the shit out of me."

"Assault" is probably the right word for Len's action. The blow was intended, powerful, and dangerous. X-rays later revealed that had the break in the bone around the occipital orb extended a fraction of an inch farther, Darren might have lost his eye. As it was, he was seriously injured by a boy whose admitted provocation had been no more than sustained verbal teasing. Moreover, Len was a big, well-muscled senior; Darren, a slight, bespectacled tenth grader. Len was a school leader, a member of the student discipline council; Darren had no official status.

To his credit, Len, whom I saw minutes after Darren was taken away to the hospital, had nothing to say in his defense. In later talks, he helped me put together a credible sequence of the teasing that had led to his finally unmanageable rage, but never—to this day—has he suggested his punch was justified, was anything other than intolerable. His remorse was, so far as I can tell, absolute. He fully expected the direst consequences: expulsion, criminal prosecution, the angriest reprisals at home. But on one point he could not have been clearer: there was no stopping him from striking that blow. As he recounted it, in the moments prior to the assault, he was unaware of anything except Darren—Darren's head, to be precise. He did not see his friend or hear his question. He cannot remember crossing the commons to Darren. Nor was there any question of deliberating on whether he would hit him or not. There was only the rage, the sighting, and the discharge of the rage.

In his defense later, his friends urged me to take into account that "Len's just not the kind of guy who could take something like that from a guy like Darren." This was true, I felt, but I told them what I told Len and his family: that he must become the kind of guy who can learn to take such blows to his esteem without a violent response. The first step, I advised, was learning to decide about anger, not merely discharging his feelings. Len paid, I believe, an appropriate price for his assault, and I hope the crisis was an occasion for learning, but I learned something too, and it has been confirmed many times since: a boy's most passionate, most forceful acts are often carried out without reflection of any kind. Boys have to do some things, even terrible things. Len knew his violence was wrong and also regrettable; but it was not, for him, avoidable. No one, in my opinion, knew this better than Darren, who at that time was undergoing a wrenchingly painful dislocation in his family. He was, I believe, hurting with the same intensity that Len was raging. Thus aggressor met victim, confirming in effect what was true of them both.

* * *

Helpless boys are not always helplessly bad. In my experience, more than a few have been helplessly good. This was strikingly true of Byron, the most wretchedly parented boy I have ever known. When I first met him,

Byron was a physically mature, provocatively sloppy ninth grader. His long black hair did not lie down, it congealed. His tired blue jeans were short enough to reveal that he wore no socks under his orange construction boots. He was heavy-lidded in a way that suggested a young hoodlum of the '50s. His voice sounded as though it came out of a long, damp pipe.

Byron's parents were separated, but lived near enough to one another that he was able to move freely — generally unnoticed — between households. His father was sullen and uncommunicative. He saw his role as disciplinarian, which for him meant periodically accusing his son of drug abuse. Byron's older brother was in the penitentiary for selling drugs. Byron's mother, in whose house he slept most nights, entertained a continuing string of boyfriends. According to Byron, there was a lot of bizarre and even dangerous sex play, especially when his mother drank too much. She too accused him of drug abuse: specifically of stealing her sedatives from the medicine chest.

Except for these accusations and other occasional derision, Byron's parents exerted little pressure on him. For instance, they did not object to (perhaps did not notice) his periodic spells of truancy, including once when he took a plane to a distant state "to see some chick."

Byron's disciplinary lapses sometimes veered into outright delinquency, but his bad behavior alternated with spurts of inspiring effort and achievement. Following his longest, most puzzling bout of truancy, he began to read tenaciously and write voluminously for a history teacher who demanded much of him. Despite his discipline scrapes, his almost theatrically beat-up appearance, and the unsavory aura of his out-of-school circumstances, Byron's freshmen classmates sensed a deep virtue in him and elected him freshman football captain. Although not a big or especially rugged boy, Byron was a tough football player—fearless. Suspended from the football team for smoking, he became a dedicated worker at the maintenance detail he was given as punishment.

In the course of these alternating lapses and surges, Byron called a colleague of mine late one night and said he had to talk to him right away. He was feeling for some reason like killing himself, and he wanted to talk. The person to whom he had reached out was the man who had disciplined him for smoking and who had supervised Byron's work detail. At the time, he had told Byron, "Why do you want to keep spoiling things by breaking petty rules? You've got too much going for you." The phrase "you've got too much going for you" struck something deep in Byron; remembering it, he said, had made him want to call my friend.

The colleague picked up Byron at his house. He was waiting alone in the kitchen, his father having driven off in anger after another accusatory row. As teacher and boy drove aimless circuits around the suburban neighborhoods, periods of silence were broken by animated disclosures from Byron about his illicit exploits, his idealistic goals, his frustration and sadness when he failed to meet them. At length, Byron calmed down, assured my friend that he would not take his life and that, if the idea arose again, he would call him right away and talk. "I know I've got a lot going for me," he said.

He would say this often during his time with us at the school. He would say it with conviction, and everyone who knew him well wanted to believe it, but his delinquencies never abated; they escalated. Even had his mother or father paid his tuition bills—and they did not—Byron would have been impossible to retain in the school. The year he was old enough to be tried as an adult, he was sent to prison for extortion. I am certain he is doing good work there.

* * *

I am also certain, because I see him from time to time, that another of my former students, Todd, is doing poor work, if he is working at all. Todd may be the most appealing, affectionate boy I have ever taught. Fine-featured, animated, nervous, he had a habit of talking around a subject until only the subject was left, chipping his way toward what was on his mind rather in the manner of a sculptor. Over the course of our acquaintance, Todd's indirection devolved into hesitant confusion, finally into a complete muddle. Like too many boys of his era, he slipped into chronic drug use and has never been able to get out.

There are no special features to his progress into dependency. A younger sibling in a large family, he did more or less what the older brothers and sister did in his chaotic, but not unloving, household. Over the summer of his first year caddying, older boys introduced him to cigarettes, and by the end of junior high school, he was sneaking out of the house with beer to share with his more daring friends. When an older brother brought some pot home, Todd, very excited, tried a pipeful. When he did not feel anything happen he was disappointed. Later, he pinched some of his brother's supply, experimented on his own, and got high.

By the time he started high school, he was getting high every day. He began organizing his plans around it, and after a time stopped making plans. By the time I got to know Todd, he was deeply unhappy with himself. He had become a marginal student and a non-participant in school life, even sports which he had once loved. But he did like to talk, and once he decided that he trusted me, he began telling me, awkwardly and concentrically, about his illicit activity. I remember the afternoon I decided to confront him about why he was disclosing his crimes to me — taking his parents' car out to drive before he had a license, leaving restaurants without paying the check. He dropped broad hints and made references to intoxication, but at this point he was unwilling to make a direct admission. "What are you doing?" I said. "Why are you telling me this?" Todd looked startled when I responded this way. He left my office that afternoon without saying goodbye.

The next day he came back and surprised me by telling me he'd been dishonest with me all along. Even the stories about the car and the restaurants were false, or mostly false. What he and his friends had been doing was actually much worse. There were real thefts, thefts of money, and the amounts were significant. He told me he drank and used marijuana. I asked him how heavily he was involved, and he said he usually got high on the weekends. I told him we had a lot to talk about. The following day he came to the office and told me he had lied about his marijuana involvement; he said he got high every day, several times.

After that Todd and I began a fairly formal program of counseling. The point of it, so far as I was concerned, was to get him to stop smoking pot, to clean the drug from his system long enough so that he would feel better and start to regain what we agreed was lost energy and capacity. The counseling began well, because Todd wanted badly to quit pot and to stop erecting the network of deceptions that went with it. For all of his street-wise delinquencies, he had set a number of conventional goals for himself: decent grades, athletic distinctions, a focal place in school activities. Failing to approach these genuinely disappointed him.

I told him we could not work together unless he gave up pot smoking at least for a "moratorium" period of six weeks. If he couldn't do that, I told him, his problem was too deep for my training. He agreed to the moratorium and I believe honestly tried to keep his commitment, but he did relapse. He confessed some of the lapses, concealed others. During this period of relative "detoxification," I worked hard to demystify the drug's sensual effects. I explained the multiple effects of cannabis's component chemicals on his system—effects he could feel immediately (the high, loss of control, cotton mouth, change of appetite); effects he could sense only vaguely (chronic upper respiratory trouble, fatigue, irregular appetite); and effects he could not feel at all. The latter, I told him, were the greatest cause for concern. We talked about the fat-solubility of tetrahydracannabinol, the chemical most responsible for pot's pleasurable high; how the THC from a single joint was absorbed in fatty tissue, including brain tissue, for weeks. I showed him photographs of cell sections from rhesus monkey brains in order to point out the difference between THC-laden, damaged cells and normal ones. Again, my goal was to make the effects of drug-taking seem concrete, real to Todd.

He didn't resist any of this. His resolve to quit, to work harder, to be more open and honest with his parents was, I am sure, sincere. But the lapses continued. At length we contacted a professional drug-abuse counselor, and Todd's work with her became a condition of his remaining in the school. Todd liked her very much and talked to me enthusiastically about his progress and how much he liked the kids in a "no-use" support group the therapist conducted several afternoons a week. Even when I was the immediate cause of his misery—for instance, when I got wind of one of his lapses, confronted him about it, and brought his parents into the picture—Todd never grew hostile. Our counseling sessions and after-school chats were animated and frequent.

He simply was, in a profound and apparently irreversible way, helpless. He and I talked often about his Catholicism, his early parochial-school training, and their possible effects on his do it, confess, do it again syndrome, and while there may have been in his case a plausible connection, his behavior was indistinguishable from that of many helpless non-Catholic boys I have known since. And like so many of them, he seemed to grow more affectionate, more disclosing, needier, the further he fell from grace.

One of the last times we talked at any length was over the summer between his undergraduate freshman and sophomore year. Although full of hope when he left home for college, he fell into really abusive drug-taking within weeks of his first term. He dropped courses, failed some, passed others on the margin. When he came to see me in June he was disgusted with himself and had, he said, several recent weeks of sobriety behind him. Moreover, he told me, he knew now that pot was his real enemy. He felt he could pass up drinking, and he had no real inclination to psychedelics or cocaine or pills. Pot, he believed, would always tempt him.

The evening following this conversation, he went to a large open-air rock concert with some friends he had not seen for almost a year. He told me later that in the car on the way to the stadium, he shared with his friends the excesses and reprisals that had marked his freshman year. He also told them about his commitment to sobriety. "Does that include pot?" they asked. He told them it did, that pot was his problem. He told me he even lectured the others at some length about the drug's long-term effects, unseen properties, etc., as he had come to understand them since we first began talking. "That may be true," the driver said, producing a bag of marijuana, "but what about this?"

"What about it?" I asked Todd when I saw him next. "What did you do?" He looked directly at me, and though he was smiling, his eyes were filling with tears.

"What do you think? I smoked. I smoked my fucking brains out."

* * *

Then there was Quint. In my experience, boys usually reveal their helplessness over time, but you had only to meet Quint once to see that he positively radiated helplessness. He was a pale black boy with an enormous "afro" the color of mercurachrome. He was powerfully muscled, physically gentle, and so soft-spoken that his breathy whisper was his trademark in the school. He slouched and, when sitting, folded into himself so that it was hard to credit that he was 7'1" tall until you actually saw him extend his frame on the basketball court. Because of his phenomenal size and at least passable agility, he was a heavily recruited high school basketball player, although his play rarely approached the expectations of coaches or fans.

Quint was a poor student, in the sense that he did not keep up with daily assignments, and he would freeze under the pressure of a tough direct question or a challenging exam. But he had a keen intuitive sense of what worked in an effective poem, what made a novelist's characterization come to life, how contemporaneous historical events fit together to define the "feel" of an era. He also sized up people surprisingly quickly and well, and his appraisals were often funny — and invariably generous.

Everybody liked Quint, but he was almost always in trouble. There was academic trouble, eligibility trouble, trouble at home; his father ran a busy restaurant in the city, and Quint seemed always either to fail to arrive or fail to perform at assigned jobs ranging from dishworker to bouncer. I taught Quint history and also talked with him often outside of class, almost always about his school troubles or home troubles. Soon after I got to know him, I was struck by how his speech would grow softer and his movements slower in proportion to the degree of his difficulties. Sometimes, at a break-down point—say, when he had forgotten to attend the detention he was assigned for forgetting to go to class—he would stop speaking and stop moving alto-gether. Inclined forward, his great arms enveloping his knees, he would stare at me imploringly, as if awaiting something unthinkable: a slap in the face, perhaps, or a bullet in the head.

I remember being called down to the basketball coach's office one day after school and finding Quint fixed in this attitude. The coach was Quint's closest adult friend in the school, and he was agitated. Quint looked at me—helplessly—when I entered the office, but he did not speak when I greeted him.

"I think we're at a dead end," the coach told me. "Quint's got a problem." The problem was complex, and it was serious. He wanted to—or at least felt obli-gated to—get married. A girl he had been seeing from his neighborhood was pregnant, and at first she had led him to believe he was the father, possibly, he thought, to induce him to marry her. Later, she had confessed that he was definitely not the father. It was this desper-ate disclosure, combined with the girl's genuinely bleak prospects, that had moved Quint to want to marry her. All of this was summarized for me by the coach. Quint, except to nod assent, said nothing.

"I told him he is throwing his life away," the coach said with feeling. He did not know what else he could say. Quint was a high school senior with a poorish scholastic record and terrible aptitude-test scores. His insight and talent were elusive and hard to quantify. But he did have a Division I basketball scholarship pending, and our hope was that this opportunity, plus some maturation, might see Quint through to adulthood. "I've tried to explain to him that there is nothing to be gained, everything to be lost, if he takes on a family at seventeen years old." The coach appealed to me. "Maybe you can tell him something I haven't."

I could see plainly that Quint was frozen, overwhelmed. I spoke to him at length and as calmly as I could. I said I appreciated that he was in a tough spot and that he had obviously thought hard about what he should do, that he had shown great kindness in being so responsive to his girlfriend's needs. I assured him I could not and would not tell him what to do. My one caution—and I gripped each of his arms to emphasize the point—was that life-shaping decisions like this should best be made slowly and deliberately. I told him I realized he must be scared and worried, but that time was on his side. Whatever he decided, I urged him not to hurry.

Before Quint left the office, the coach and I offered him every kind of help we could think of. We offered to help the girl and her baby, within the limits of our means. We gave him the name of a good physician. We said we would be on call if he wanted to talk more later, and we gave him our home phone numbers to take with him. As he rose to go, Quint spoke at last. He said, "Thanks a lot. This really helped. I think I'm starting to see what to do." He gave us a broad, sad smile and left.

Quint did not return to school for several days. We did not hear from him, and he could not be reached at home. At length his father called from the restaurant with the news that Quint had somehow managed to get married. In fact, we learned that he had been married shortly after leaving the office.

Evil Boys

Esther, the stout and stoical woman in charge of the school's housekeeping, might be said to have seen it all with respect to the dark side of boys' nature. Working alone at night in the empty school building, she often had the first adult glimpse of the vilest epithets committed to desk or locker face or toilet stall. Graffiti slogans are usually predictable, merely vulgar. But sometimes their angry or pornographic messages carry a special power: a kind of exhilarating self-disgust.

In one particularly vicious graffiti campaign against a boy whose sexuality was being impugned, the vandal literally filled the inner walls of a toilet stall with "Wentling sucks." The sheer extent of the scrawl undid Esther, and she could not bring herself to stay in that polluted space and scour the walls clean. When she told the dean about it the next day, he was sympathetic and offered to do it himself. But as it happened, Esther fortified herself and returned to the lavatory to finish the job. After all, she had cleaned up the worst messes imaginable: smears of excrement; nose effluence; vomit; lockers in which food had been left to putrify; reeking underwear and socks. Upon entering the stall, however, she found that the graffitist had returned, and the message stopped her short. To each slogan was added, in the same hand, "and swallows."

Esther's worst moment on the job, however, was occasioned by another, far more grotesque instance of graffiti. This one, I know, hastened her retirement. One winter evening she entered the boys' lavatory to find "Satan Wills & Satan Kills" smeared over the mirrors, sinks, and tiles—apparently in blood. Her voice shaking, she called me at home. I drove directly to school and found her still upset.

Under the whitening fluorescent lights, the scene in the lavatory was unsettling. The words did look as if they were composed of blood, deep reds dried to brown and black, but I wanted to believe it was paint, that some overwrought, ornery fan of Stephen King had attempted a showy prank. But if it was indeed blood, it was quite a lot of blood. I called the police, who came promptly, took a report from Esther, photographed the messages, and scraped off some samples to be analyzed. Then we washed the sinks and mirrors and tiles clean. The next morning the police called to confirm that the writing had indeed been in blood—human blood. I alerted guidance staff about what had happened, but no one had a clue as to who might have done such a thing, and the effect of my report was decidedly depressing.

We never found out who wrote the slogans in blood on the lavatory walls. Nor did the writer stop. Throughout that winter and spring, perhaps once every six weeks, another slogan would appear, sickening in its appearance: "Satan likes this," "Satan, yes," "Good Satan blood." Usually the smears appeared in the lavatory, but one appeared on the wall of the corridor where humanities courses are taught, another on the glass of the doors to the entrance of the school. The fact that the incidents ended with that school year in June suggested a senior was most likely the blood-writer.

The mind turns naturally on unsolved mysteries, and this one had an upsetting effect on the few of us who knew about it. Some boy had let his blood, a copious amount if it, and had linked his blood-letting to Satan. This was certainly pathology, and some actual boy in our midst was acting it out. But if I am honest I would confess that what irritated me most about these incidents was their unavoidable invitation to consider that sheer hell—evil itself—was at loose in the school.

It is not for nothing that children, almost always boys, are sometimes said to "raise hell," certain types to be "hellraisers." Ours is a secular age, and being a cliché both blurs and lightens the metaphor, but raising—realizing—hell is precisely what boys do when they are held in a certain kind of thralldom. The Canadian novelist Robertson Davies documents that capacity vividly in *The Manticore*, the first volume of his *Deptford Trilogy*.

A group of teenage boys freed from their summer camp break into the empty vacation home of an elderly couple. The boys are a little reticent to trespass and, at first, to take part in acts of vandalism. But a darkly infectious impulse to mayhem is imparted by the group leader, Bill Unsworth. Before long, breakable keepsakes are shattered, books ripped apart, furniture demolished with a crowbar. But even this is not enough for Bill Unsworth, who assembles a mound of family memorabilia, including children's photographs, on the dining room table. Then he climbs atop the table, drops his trousers, and squats over the mound to defecate. What follows is rivetingly horrible, even to—especially to—the fellow delinquents, one of whom narrates:

How long it took I cannot tell, but they were critical moments in my life. For as he struggled, red-faced and pop-eyed, and as he appeared at last with a great stool dangling from his ape-like rump, I regained my senses and said to myself, not "What am I doing here?" but "Why is he doing that?" The destruction was a simple prelude to this. It is a dirty, animal act of defiance and protest against—well, against what? He doesn't even know who these people are. There is no spite in him against individuals who have injured him. Is he protesting against order, against property, against privacy? No; there is nothing intellectual, nothing rooted in principle—even the principle of anarchy—in what he is doing. So far as I can judge—and I must remember that I am his accomplice in all but this, his final outrage—he is simply being as evil as his strong will and deficient imagination will permit. He is possessed, and what possesses him is evil.[19]

I have known boys who have been evil, or at least who were possessed by it. The first to come to mind is Colin, a strikingly handsome, wolfish-looking boy who played football and lacrosse, so far as I could tell, to hurt opposing players. There is a kind of licit contact, an attitude in checking or tackling, that can convey hatred, exploit frustration. Those games allow proximities and intimacies in which intolerable insult and aggression can be voiced, unheard by anyone save the intended target. Colin had a genius for these opportunities. And while he got into an outsized share of trouble, in sports and otherwise, he typically "drew" the foul, the counter-curse, the flail of punches from a seething opponent. Athletic officials often see only the dramatic response to a subtle provocation; Colin knew that his victims' rage was aggravated by their helpless inability to prove this. He was a boy gangs would form to destroy. When they tried, Colin skillfully manipulated police and other authorities to intervene. In ways they could not articulate, Colin's classmates and teammates feared him, but they felt powerless, somehow ashamed, to express it. Many were more than willing to keep his company, perhaps stimulated by the aura of unpredictable danger that always seemed to surround him.

He dissembled without any apparent motive, bore bad, insulting news with relish. "Lou, you're cut!" he'd shout across the student commons to an unsuccessful team candidate who had not yet seen the roster. To a classmate known to have a hopeless crush on Cindy, he would confide "I just heard Cindy's going to the prom with Pete, which cracks me up because Pete thinks she's a total dog." To boys self-consciously slender ("still lifting, Chet?") or pudgy ("Keep wearing those tight shirts, you're looking good") or small ("Your mother know you're out so late?") or broken out with acne, ("Time for a little soap and water, hey?") he was unerringly devastating. He was especially inventive in creating animosity among faculty:

Colin:	Hey, Miss Stevens, Mr. Douglas thinks you're an easy grader.
Miss Stevens:	Oh, does he?
Colin:	That's what he says.
Miss Stevens:	Well, we all can't have Mr. Douglas's high standards.

* * *

Colin:	Hey, Mr. Douglas, Miss Stevens just burned you.
Mr. Douglas:	Oh, did she? How did she 'burn' me?
Colin:	No offense sir, but I think she thinks you're kind of . . . pompous.
Mr. Douglas:	She thinks I'm pompous?
Colin:	Yeah. She says things like "We all can't have Mr. Douglas's high standards." The

	way she says it is, you know, kind of a put-down.
Mr. Douglas:	I'm glad Miss Stevens feels she can confide in you, Colin.
Colin:	Hey, no offense. I'm pretty surprised myself that she would say a thing like that. It seems awfully cold, for a teacher.

Perhaps once every term Colin would seek out a new boy in the school, pay him unexpected attention. Invariably the boy chosen was socially isolated, physically or otherwise awkward, needy. He was usually, but not always, a year or more younger than Colin. Though widely known to be a bad boy, Colin was also instinctively recognized by everyone as a significant person in the school. To a tentative and unpopular boy, Colin's forcefulness could be irresistible. Even his teasing, even his deadpan put-downs could appeal to a boy hungry enough for recognition.

Colin courted such souls, although there appeared to be no sexual aim or feeling in either pursuit or conquest. The emotional pay off seemed to lie solely in creating a clear dependency on the part of the new "friend." To non-drivers, Colin offered rides. He found female partners for boys who had never dated. He took his wide-eyed initiates to parties: illicit gatherings in houses of students whose parents had departed for the weekend. The credible bearer of false I.Ds, Colin introduced his initiates to drinking games, to equivocal taverns. When the novice drinker got drunk and sick, Colin was solicitous, covering for him, improvising late-night sleep-overs, so that parents would not behold a drunken son.

These manipulations were devastatingly, transparently effective. Seasoned companions of Colin would see at once that a new conquest was in the making. Some watched it develop with fascination, others played along actively. Inevitably Colin would voice derision and contempt for the initiate, would suddenly distance himself from him, then spurn him altogether.

For the abandoned boy, the surprise, the incomprehension, and the ensuing humiliation could be unendurable. One such victim, a pudgy, sputtering tenth grader named Ezra, was taken up by Colin in the usual half-joshing, half-affectionate way as the lacrosse team's unofficial mascot. By no means a player, Ezra was nonetheless an enthusiast. Colin convinced Ezra to serve as the team manager, and Ezra slavishly complied. Colin drove the dazzled Ezra home from practice, inserted Ezra in the otherwise off-limits and "senior section" of the locker area, an enclave of jocks and "party-ers" where even many seniors were not welcome. Colin initiated Ezra to drinking, and Ezra's drunken antics were the talk of the lacrosse team. Away from Colin and his crowd, Ezra affected a new, unnatural swagger, a close-lipped knowingness that appalled his classmates.

As it happened, Ezra's association with Colin almost killed him. When he learned Ezra's parents were going out of town, leaving him on his own, Colin easily

persuaded him to have a weekend party. There may
have been some objection, but Colin's urgings were
irresistible. Colin himself broadcast news of the party
throughout the student body and beyond. Moreover,
on the appointed Friday, he brought a case of beer to
Ezra's house hours before the party was to begin. By
the time the first carloads of students arrived, Ezra was
falling-down, sick drunk. Colin greeted the guests at
the door, pointing out the staggering, incoherent Ezra
as if he were an exhibit.

Ezra flew into a rage that no one could interpret.
When he started flailing his fists, Colin forced him to
the floor and sat on his chest. As he spoke to him in his
deadpan drawl, "What's the problem, Ezra? You're not
making a whole lot of sense tonight, Ezra," another boy
stooped down and poured a bottle of beer into Ezra's
gasping mouth. When he was released, Ezra got up,
stumbled into the back pantry, punched his fist
through a window and reflexively withdrew it, cutting
open the length of his forearm.

When Ezra, lying in a mess of his own vomit and
blood, was spotted sometime later, Colin spread the
word and the crowd stampeded out of the house and
into their cars. Someone mercifully dialled 911 before
leaving Ezra's house, and his life was saved. He had
nearly bled to death. The hospital determined that his
blood alcohol level was between toxic and lethal. Colin
never spoke to Ezra again.

Perhaps there is a sinister social dynamic at work
in any sizable grouping of school-age boys. And perhaps the critical size is not very great; a dozen or so
boys stranded on a remote island was sufficient for evil

to come murderously into play in William Golding's *Lord of the Flies*. A summer camp, or even a camp cabin, a school, club, fraternity, gang—any and each of these might be a fertile culture for the evil in boys. Boys like Colin are, in a sense and for a time, monstrous; they are also everywhere at hand.

* * *

Some boys are so exaggeratedly hell-bent, so helplessly in the adrenal thrall of badness, that when they and their actions are set down plainly in words, they strain credulity. Because they do, their dreadfulness is generally denied. Among more affluent and educated circles, the denial is often couched in facile psychological terms: perhaps "character disordered," "high risk behavior pattern," or "passive aggressive" syndrome.

Every year I come to know a boy or boys who shatter such glib formulations like china. Bad boys of fiction seldom rival real ones. It would almost certainly strain a fiction reader's credulity to meet Tyler, a boy who at sixteen evoked dread in everybody who came to know him. No one, least of all his parents, could recall a time when he was not, literally, dreadful. As a preschooler he revealed an abiding preoccupation with the horrible, especially spiders and reptiles. This fascination was skittishly indulged by his family who hoped it might develop into something improving, possibly zoological research. This development never occurred. However, Tyler did continue to keep tarantulas, scorpions, and boa constrictors. His emotional investment in these creatures consisted in feeding them living prey and exhibiting them unexpectedly to whoever was likely to be most terrified. "How big are your snakes?" I asked him once, when I learned he kept boa constrictors. "They're getting big enough to kill you," he said, smiling but not joking.

Killing and hurting people dominated Tyler's conversation. He became a relentless cagey bully, and he took special pleasure in threatening younger boys. His threats had far more power than teasing; they came from a boy who kept scorpions and tarantulas and ten-foot snakes. By the end of junior high school, his bullying had become generalized into more broadly anti-social behavior. He became a self-styled bigot, drawing symbols and voicing slogans of the Nazis and the Klu Klux Klan. When these were detected, parents were advised, diagnostic tests administered, a succession of child therapists put to work. In consequence, Tyler seemed only to grow meaner.

Tyler was expelled from school his sophomore year. There had been an unbroken stream of disciplinary infractions from bullying to petty vandalism to smoking. His expulsion followed his repeated racial harassment of two black classmates. Tyler defiantly denied every allegation, even when his slurs were widely witnessed. A week after he was dismissed, he made his way on foot back to school and struck one such witness in the back with a tire iron. The police were called, and they took Tyler away, spitting and cursing, in a squad car. The following year, he made his way back to our campus again — again with automotive tools. Undetected, he managed to make his way to the previously assaulted boy's car, loosen the nuts holding the front wheels in place, and sneak off. That afternoon the car's owner sensed something seriously wrong as he made his way home from school. A faint wobble grew increasingly severe, and just as he applied his breaks, his right front wheel dropped off, dipping one of his axles to the pavement. When the tow truck attendant noted the suspicious loosening of the car's other wheel nuts, police were called. A week earlier, there had been a similar accident in a car driven by a girl in Tyler's new school. The girl had given Tyler's name to the police as a likely suspect. They investigated, but found no conclusive evidence that he had done it—although he did admit to having written her a note telling her she would die, as, he said, a joke. The boy whose car had been tampered with also indicated Tyler as a possible suspect and recounted the previous year's assault. Pressure mounted, and in time a boy Tyler had confided in told the police that Tyler had committed both crimes—and several others. After a search of his house revealed thousands of dollars worth of stolen goods, criminal tools, weapons, explosives, and illegal drugs, Tyler was sent away to a correctional school. Before he left, he sent word to several boys and girls that he would be back, and that when he returned they would wish they had never been born.

Tyler was, incidentally, a well-coordinated boy of ordinary size, with a strong scholastic testing profile. His family was moderately well-to-do and lived in a semi-rural development of attractive houses. He had short sandy hair, regular features, clear complexion, and arresting grey blue eyes. He had, in repose, the face of an angel.

UNWORLDLY BOYS

In his superbly thoughtful book, *Secret Gardens*,[20] Humphrey Carpenter makes a persuasive case that the profusion of transformingly powerful children's books that appeared in the decades spanning Queen Victoria's reign and the first world war was a kind of collective elegy for a lost world. At the highest level of generality, the lost world is childhood itself, and refinding it fantastically or whimsically as the young heroes and heroines do in *Alice in Wonderland, Peter Pan, Wind in the Willows, The Secret Garden, The Water Babies,* or *Winnie the Pooh* has proved durably appealing to children. Carpenter also suggests that something more specific than childhood passed with the Victorian era. For the writers in question, predominantly men, something arcadian, something pastoral and fine passed as well. The child's spiritual link with the green earth — with water and meadow in particular — seemed forever severed by the ultimate and massive encroachment of city, industry, and internal combustion. From the vantage point of the great children's-story writers, a vernal past they had just managed to glimpse and to savor had been effaced by modernism. The military-industrial ravages of World War I killed it forever.

Carpenter's thesis is that not just the likes of Alice

or Peter Pan or Ratty or Mole needed pastoral sweet-
ness—a prior, better time—in order to thrive; so did
their creators. So do, my school experience suggests,
many boys. Certain boys, even as I write, seem to have
emerged into an era that is cruelly inappropriate to
their distinctive spirit and gifts.

Donald Merritt was such a boy. He came to us
midway through high school when his elegant family
was transferred to this city by the corporation which
employed his father. There had been many such
moves, at least seven or eight of them, in the course of
Donald Merritt's schooling, and he had learned to ac-
commodate these dramatic changes of context with a
flourish. In fact, Donald Merritt did everything with a
flourish.

From the moment he was introduced to the assembled school as a new boy entering mid-year, his
classmates were at a loss as to what to make of him. He
was tall and willowy, and his longish blond hair fell
away from a center part in untidy curls. Whatever
complicated shirt and jersey arrangement he happened
to be wearing, the effect was always of some kind of
buccaneer's blouse. His black woolen cape—quickly to
become Donald's trademark in the school—was, the
morning he was introduced, draped jauntily over one
arm.

His almost ridiculously Byronic demeanor, it
turned out, took no inspiration from Lord Byron.
When I got to know Donald, I asked him about Byron,
and he cheerfully drew a blank. I was not far wrong,
however, suspecting there was an historical figure be-

hind Donald's swashbuckling persona. That figure, as it happened, was Rimbaud, the French imagist poet and famous enfant terrible. Donald Merritt was encyclopedic about Rimbaud. He could cite whole poems in both English and French. The French was intoned nasally and boldly, the accent wildly inaccurate. In fact, a French teaching colleague claimed that these impromptu recitations were indecipherable as French. But to the ears of his fellow students, Donald's utterances from Rimbaud were sufficiently "foreign" to impress.

Donald also knew seemingly every detail of Rimbaud's dissolute, foreshortened life. In my own classroom, he once reported at length about Rimbaud's troubled love affair with his fellow *imagiste*, Paul Verlaine. When other boys expressed uneasy interest in the lovers' homosexuality or drug-taking, Donald was loftily contemptuous. "That is a very American, very middle class question," he chided one questioner. Rimbaud and Verlaine were, in his words, destructively, brutally true to their art. "The poems more than justify the lives," he would say, then declaim in forceful nasal tones what may have been "The Drunken Boat."

Donald was apparently unfazed in any way by the masculine teenage conventions of his classmates. If his posturing was an act, it was a flawless act. I can still picture him when the bell sounded ending the instructional day: cutting a swashbuckling path through the throngs of boys heading down to pool or gym or mat for afternoon practices. Donald's leonine head of curls would be thrown back, his cape flung back over his shoulder, as the student body coursed past him like weather.

His senior year he expressed some interest in a play I had decided to direct that winter: Edgar Lee Masters' *Spoon River Anthology*. He told me he had acted in the play previously, in Minneapolis, and that the performance had been staged in an actual cemetery among the graves. "And that," he told me "is how it should really be done." I did not agree, and in any event I could not imagine such a performance in the dead of winter in Cleveland, Ohio. Whatever reservations he felt about participating in a possibly workaday production of the play, Donald surprised me by auditioning. Up to that point, he had made a point of disdaining all of the school's extra-curricular activities. He liked to leave the school at the earliest allowable hour in order, his schoolmates presumed, to get on with whatever Rimbaud-like activity was available beyond our gates.

More surprising than his decision to try out for *Spoon River Anthology* was the quality of his audition. Although he read loudly and clearly, he was a wooden and painfully unnatural presence on stage. To my pleas to act more naturally and to declaim less, he seemed quietly exasperated. "It was very different in Minneapolis," he said more than once. In the course of an extensive audition it became clear to me that Donald would not be able to play a role in *Spoon River*. He read the lines of an unrequited lover, a town drunk, and a severe clergyman in exactly the same strident voice, rather as if he were shouting detailed instructions from a hilltop to faraway listeners.

If Donald was disappointed at not being cast, he did not let on. He did attend the performance, however, and sought me out afterward to tell me, "You really have to see this play in a cemetery."

Donald Merritt was not a very strong student, even in the arts and humanities courses in which his familiarity with artists and writers unknown to his classmates might have been thought to give him a scholastic edge. The consensus of his teachers was that Donald, while reasonably bright, did very little schoolwork. His compositions tended to be surprisingly general, grandiose, thin in substance.

Recommending Donald to college was tricky, because his teachers wanted to stress his individuality and its undeniably stimulating effect on school life, but there was also an honorable reluctance to overpraise a boy of largely unfulfilled promise. Some colleagues felt that Donald was a superficial scholar and at best a kind of eccentric impostor. But whatever doubts the faculty had about his prospects, they were not shared by college admissions officers. His distinctive bearing and turnout, his interest in Rimbaud and the imagists, his extensive travels, and his collection of Venetian glass ornaments combined to make him an irresistibly attractive applicant. His modest SAT scores, 'C' average, and the mild reservations of some of his teachers were cast aside in the face of such a distinctive approach to teenage life.

To the consternation of a few hardworking classmates who were not so chosen, Donald Merritt was admitted to Yale. A veteran admissions officer there told me, almost derisively, that Donald was the first really interesting boy he had interviewed from my school.

I don't know if Donald blazed a distinctive trail through New Haven. I learned only that he left the university after a term. Reports differed as to the reason. Some said he was unhappy at Yale from the start; others that he had done almost no work, had virtually flunked out. Moreover, I heard that Donald did not return to his family, but had taken off, to travel, destination unknown.

For eight years I did not hear another word from or about Donald, and then I learned he had died of AIDS. Before he got ill, he apparently made a substantial reputation for himself as a sculptor. An alumnus of the school who runs a gallery in St. Louis sent me a handsomely printed book-length catalog of Donald's work, exhibits photographed from a posthumous show. I cannot judge the sculptures: large, column-like forms in polished metal. They resembled human torsos, or, some of them, tree trunks. The catalog also included selected writings from a journal Donald kept. From these I learned that he had changed his name to Merritt St. John. About his AIDS symptoms he wrote, "It is true, I feel this way, this no-energy way, but it can't be true! There have been and there continue to be so many beautiful people. Living people. This day and this sky are so clean, so bright, so beautiful. There has got to be something to learn in this sickness, something great, even in this."

* * *

Years after Donald Merritt left the school, another unworldly boy, Lance, emerged in our midst. Too much time had elapsed for him to have known anything about Donald, but I know Lance would have idolized him. By the time he was midway through high school, Lance had become something of an idol himself.

Lance did not wear period costumes, except when he was acting on stage, but he managed to make a costume out of even the most conventional clothes. It would not convey the truth to say that he was "beautifully dressed," because he was too beautifully dressed. He wore the kind of clothes other boys wore, and on that account I suppose he was fashionable; but on him clothes seemed somehow to glow. His boating moccasins appeared to be always new and glossily oiled, the pristine white soles unstained by turf. Corduroys and khakis, pressed to blade-like creases, broke luxuriantly over shoe top. His button-down shirts could have been catalog advertisements for good cloth. The deep greens and blues of his pullovers, the tartan plaids of hunting shirts were distractingly vivid and rich. This perfection of turn-out — hair, posture, attitude, clothing — was frequently intolerable, yet endlessly fascinating, to his classmates. I had to discipline a boy once for saying in class, "Lance, how come you always look like something from out of a store?"

Not that Lance would have been bothered much by such a remark. Narcissistic as it may have been, Lance's habit of dress was no brittle defense. He was bone-comfortable in his beautiful duffle coats and vividly striped college scarves. He was bone-comfortable, period. Smiley, clean, immaculately groomed, he never expressed a trace of irritability or meanness. His manner of speaking was purringly effeminate, but because he was quick and very funny, he came in for surprisingly little schoolboy derision; there was no point in teasing him. Lance was generous in his judgments of his classmates, and he was also generous with his time and his possessions. He was a well-prepared scholar, a gifted actor, and a hopeless non-athlete, although he played gently at golf and tennis, looking gleamingly right in the clothes.

Girls adored Lance and pursued him, literally, in swarms. Whenever he spoke in assembly or was otherwise likely to be in the public gaze, the school's atmosphere of male sanctuary was likely to be broken by the giddy intrusion of a dozen or so of Lance's coltish girl friends. Female auditions for school plays swelled to three or four times the ordinary number if Lance was also rumored to be trying out. For opening-night performances, almost the entire auditorium seemed to be peopled with girls awaiting a glimpse of Lance.

To be accurate, it was not simply a glimpse of Lance they came for—or what, for that matter, appealed to audiences generally. They came to see Lance transformed. Sure and total personal transformation was his genius. He was always effective as a character from a remote historical era—say, as one of Sir Thomas More's ecclesiastical enemies in *Man for all Seasons* or some ardent Shakespearian suitor. But a few times Lance brought his roles to so high a cathartic pitch that his communion with his audience transformed them. This happened when he played a character he seemed born to play, someone fay and charming and airily insubstantial: Ernest in *The Importance of Being Earnest* or Beverly Carleton in *The Man Who Came to Dinner*. In these roles, he communicated a frivolity so preposterous and so delightful that his audience—his girls especially—convulsed and squealed in advance of his comic punch lines. When this pitch had been established, Lance's mere entrance on stage would stir a hum of anticipation.

Without a trace of counterfeit accent, Lance somehow found the class and period of these eloquent, unflappable dandies, his performance glitteringly professional on a stage full of what were otherwise merely attractive teenagers. Where did the voice, the intonation, the manner, the pocket handkerchief, his ease with a cane come from? Not, certainly, from his cheerful middle-class suburban family. Not from any specialized taste for classic books or films or plays; his knowledge of drama and literature outside the school curriculum was modest. Nor did his perfect pitch, his timing, his nuances come from knowing direction. I directed Lance a few times myself, and he always brought his character to rehearsal fully realized.

The answer lay, I believe, in a deep need and a deep talent for transformation. Lance sensed that art transformed the commonplace. The most complete transformations were those that replaced one's whole in-this-world personality: characters created on the stage. And the greatest characters were playful, undangerous wizards, people like Oscar Wilde or his Ernest, who were not so much artificial as artifice itself. Playing that role on stage, Lance was incandescent.

And again, even off the stage, even in a history classroom you sensed Lance's power to transform himself
from schoolboy to something more rarefied; you
sensed it in those glowing clothes.

* * *

Bull Becker never performed in a school play,
although by the time he appeared in my classroom as a
ninth grader, he had assumed a character that would
have played wonderfully in any number of shows. He
was a sturdy little block of a boy with thick black hair
brushed back in a kind of pompadour. His family had
nicknamed him "Bull" when he was a baby, but the
boys at their comic, cruel best could not have tagged
him more aptly. Bull was a driven person. His face was
fixed invariably in an expression hovering between irritation and ferocity. His stocky form inclined forward
when he walked, conveying further the impression of
extreme determination. I was never able to learn where
his particular clothing obsession came from; there was
clearly no influence from the world of his peers. It is
probably safe to say that no other youth in the past
century has ever voluntarily turned himself out the
way Bull Becker did.

He wore only dark blue suits, usually with a
matching vest. Occasionally, at Christmas perhaps, he
would wear a plaid or a bright red waistcoat instead of
the blue one. His shirts were always white and heavily
starched, his ties solid red or black. Toting his old-
fashioned leather brief case, initialed BB in gold, Bull
moved through hallway traffic in the manner of a min-

iature accountant or mortician. Because he was such a startling oddity at school, he was sometimes a figure of fun. But only sometimes. His very intensity carried with it a kind of forcefulness. His seriousness was often taken seriously.

Bull was a moderately good student: well-organized, quick to see the point under consideration, but he rarely took an assignment beyond what was required. Essays tended to be correct but terse. In one avenue of academic life he was uncharacteristically expansive. Any discussion of current politics drew his rapt attention and evoked from him remarkably well informed analysis.

He was passionately, unswervingly conservative. He thought governments should be small, as non-regulatory as possible, their civic activity limited to judicial and police functions. He felt government at every level had become bloated with expendable bureaucrats who tended to look after their own interests rather than those they claimed to serve. "As a business," he said, "the U.S. postal service is a disgrace." He had even harsher things to say of the state driver's license bureau. He believed the country had become since the '30s a welfare state and that it was corrupt, wasteful, and unproductive. He despised taxes as the worst imaginable means of building roads and schools or redistributing wealth.

Bull Becker was also radically martial. He was for a bristling national-weapons arsenal, and he favored nonnuclear weapons, weapons you could actually fire and use. He approved of unilateral, immediate retaliation for any act of terrorism, for breaches of treaties, or for any other foreign gesture hostile to the national interest. He was against abortion, against affirmative action, and he wanted the draft reinstated. About these and other political issues he was impressively well read. He backed up his views with facts, with names, with examples, with reference to specific precedent.

Once a city councilman speaking to the student body bemoaned the paltry commitment of funds that had been made to Cleveland's beleaguered public schools. When it was time for questions from the audience, Bull Becker was on his feet. There was plenty of money allocated to Cleveland schools, he said, naming a figure of several thousand dollars per pupil annually. It was an amount surpassing that allocated for other, demonstrably more effective public systems, and it was an amount exceeding the cost of a good private school, including ours. Where was the money going? he asked. Why, he asked further, was twice as much money being paid to union boiler operators in the Cleveland Schools than was being paid to good teachers; those senior boiler operators, he pointed out, earned more — and he named the figure — than his headmaster. The councilman was neither quick nor effective in response. He hedged and stuttered. He questioned the dollar per pupil figure Bull had cited. Bull answered sharply that the figure was a matter of public record and was published in *The Cleveland Plain Dealer*. The councilman went on to speak of complexities in the system, of unseen costs. He convinced no one. Bull carried the point.

Bull also carried the point, but devastatingly, the day an anti-war drama troupe came to school to mount a play illustrating the folly of spending scarce resources on building weapons of unthinkable destructive power. I thought the play was fairly good. The plot followed the plight of a seemingly naive housewife who, using no more than household common sense, builds a humane case against the missiles that are stored near the town where she lives. The play made Bull furious.

There was an open discussion period afterward in which students and faculty were invited to engage the troupe, including the writer, in discussion and argument about the issues raised in the play. Bull was first to speak: was the troupe advocating unilateral disarmament? The answer was a guarded yes: that the U.S.A. should take at least the first steps toward disarmament, discontinuing certain weapons as a sign of good faith, then negotiating further steps mutually. Bull asked them if there had been a single instance of such unilateral gestures working to advance peace in the past century. He then unleashed a torrent of examples in which Hitler's Germany and Cold War Russia had answered pacific gestures with martial ones, resulting always in a military advantage for the aggressor. Where is the indication the Communist-bloc nations want peace? Who are the actual figures who want and would negotiate such a peace? The actors grew hesitant, their discussion techniques—"That's an interesting point, what do some of you others think?" "You sound very concerned—where are these feelings coming from?"—failed to reverse the direction of Bull's interrogation. Bull was on a tear. The audience was riveted to the conflict.

Finally, a member of the troupe broke in and said, "You're asking a lot of questions. Let me ask you one. Are you for war?" Bull narrowed his eyes. "No one is for war for its own sake," he said. "But there are things a person should fight for, and there are things a nation should fight for. I would fight for freedom and for fairness, and I'd fight against anybody who denied those things or took them away. How about you? What would you fight for?" The actor said, "I'm not a fighter." "I hope you feel thankful," Bull said, rising, "that there are people willing to do your fighting for you. Because if there weren't such people, you wouldn't be free to go around putting on this little play. I don't think I have anything more to say to you." Bull left the auditorium.

Probably because he had doubts about his country's resolve to arm and defend itself, and thus him, Bull built up a little arsenal of his own. He started collecting weapons when he was a small boy, at first facsimiles of antique pistols, muskets, breech-loading rifles. Then, when he was old enough to go hunting with his father, he began acquiring working rifles and pistols. When not in use or out being cleaned and oiled, Bull's guns were kept in locked glass display cases illuminated with their own small light bulbs. There was something irrational, even a little crazed, about Bull's preoccupation with these guns and their lethal capacity. Classmates who knew about the arsenal teased him about it. They mocked him, called him "The Enforcer," "Bull Eastwood." Some students were genuinely concerned about Bull's possession of actual guns and ammunition. "He's so weird," one boy confided to me. "You go over to his house, and that's all he wants to do, show you his guns, take them out and handle them." His classmates' teasing, their failure to share his obsession with the beautiful firearms hurt him more deeply than he let on. I believe he hoped the guns might serve as a basis of mutual interest, even of friendship. Bull Becker had never in his life had a friend, although I didn't learn this until much later, after Bull had endured many troubles and had undergone many changes.

About midway through his high school career Bull created something of a sensation at school by declaring openly, to any and all who would listen, that he was gay. I do not honestly know whether news like this carries a greater emotional impact in an all-boys school; it probably does. Whatever they may have written on a questionnaire, the boys' opinions of homosexuality ranged, in my opinion, from frightened hostility and disgust (a minority) to genuine or willed acceptance (a minority) to a determined unwillingness to think specifically about it (vast majority). Bull made it very hard on the latter group, because he made so many public utterances on the subject. He turned any essay assignments he could to a consideration of his homosexuality or of homosexuality generally. He wrote letters to the school paper and to the Cleveland papers identifying himself as a gay man. He joined an active gay-support group and began subscribing to gay publications.

His comparatively elderly and staid parents were paralyzed with embarrassment at Bull's disclosure. When asked to come to school to discuss the situation, they were certain that Bull would be expelled, an outcome to which they were fully resigned. But the idea of expelling Bull never came up. The only disruption of school life that resulted from his "coming out" was the stir that arose after Bull declared that he was "in love with" Steven Mix, the stalwart and amiable president of the Student Judicial Council.

Bull's declaration of love for Steven Mix made thrilling, sensational, hilarious news among the students. Moreover, it directed what might have been unbearable pressure on Steven, were it not for his remarkably graceful response. Tall, bespectacled, serious-minded, Steven Mix had been one of a few boys in the school who, while not a friend of Bull's, had never belittled or shunned him. Steven took Bull's political views — even, to some extent, Bull himself — seriously.

Steven was comfortable enough with himself to parry the Bull-related kidding directed at him. His much talked about "answer" to Bull's declaration of love had an unquestionably positive, educative effect on the school. Not long after the fact, Bull himself told me what Steven had actually said to him. He said: "I don't really know what to tell you, Bull, because I'm not gay myself. I guess I'm flattered, though." This amorous, but not personal, rebuff somehow reflected favorably on both boys.

"I don't know what I expected," Bull confided later. "But what's the point in feeling something like that if you never let the other person know?"

In Bull's remaining time in the school, not everyone was as delicately respectful as Steven Mix had been. Bull's general eccentricity no doubt exacerbated the crueler sexual teasing he endured, mostly from younger boys. Although in some ways, his peculiar manner also mitigated the stigma of his announced sexual difference. He was not a stereotypical homosexual; and he was by no means effeminate. In truth it was hard to think of Bull in terms of gender. He was still just Bull, a solitary fire plug of a boy in dark blue suits.

That is, he was Bull. About a year after his graduation, there was a rumor that he had changed dramatically. Then I saw him—playing the drums for a summer-stock musical—and realized it was true. At first, I could barely recognize him. He had grown enough so that he was almost tall, and he had thinned out. He still wore his black hair brushed back, but it had somehow relaxed, perhaps because it was longer, framing loosely what had become a rather appealing man's face.

Sitting at his drum set (where had he learned to play drums? To play them professionally well?), he was a vision of languid comfort. He wore a black golf shirt open at the neck and, I think, jeans. But the unforgettable difference in his appearance was the smile. He smiled a broad, privately absorbed smile as he played. The smile was livelier, more animated when he sought me out and chatted for a moment after the show. His manner was easy now, and he laughed a lot. Yes, he was liking school, he said, a great place, great people.

That summer, too, the word among Bull's classmates was that he was not gay. Was he ever gay? Who knows. He is big now, comfortable and loose. There is that easy, knowing smile, and the only continuous feature of the driven, forward-leaning little Bull and the languid young man at the drum set is a hint of the old forcefulness: enough compressed energy, enough life to create self after surprising self.

* * *

There are unworldly boys. Some of them, too many of them seem uncomfortable in their very skin.

Trevor Diggs was such a person. He was a black boy whose lightly complected skin was stretched like parchment over the sharp bones of his cheeks and chin. He was so emaciated, so teeteringly slender that it was almost impossible to disengage your gaze from his form. The sharp angles of his face were accented by the pointed tips of his ears, so that in a strangely coherent way Trevor Diggs looked like some elfin creation of the illustrator Arthur Rackham.

Shortly after Trevor entered the school, we learned that he was actually, and not just apparently, emaciated. In fact, he had been diagnosed as having anorexia nervosa, an eating disorder rare in males. Anorexic subjects tend to starve themselves, and the drive is very difficult to reverse. We learned of Trevor's anorexia after he was absent from school for an alarmingly long time. An aunt, who served as Trevor's guardian, came in to explain Trevor's diagnosis. She explained his symptoms and the program of counseling that her physician had recommended. Trevor had been anorexic, she believed, for two years. The symptoms commenced immediately after his younger sister was raped. The attack had occurred in the corridor of his aunt's apartment house. Trevor and his sister were in transit from the school bus to the apartment, where Trevor's afternoon duties were to look after her until his aunt came home from work. Roughed up and threatened himself, Trevor had witnessed the attack in helpless terror. Afterward, in addition to his eating disorder, Trevor's already solicitous attention to his sister became obsessive. He had, as he said, "been in charge."

My own impression was that Trevor had from

childhood been a dutiful, almost obsessively well behaved boy. The violation of his sister convinced him that he had not been good enough. His drive to be good, to be ever better, seemed to burn visibly within him. Meeting him for the first time, you would be struck by a strange, unsettling quality. He was so gentle, yet so driven. The effect of his presence on me, even before I knew anything about him, was to make me feel vaguely guilty: somehow compromised, too comfortable.

Although the focus of considerable attention, Trevor actively tried to avoid it. Fervently religious—Catholic—he spoke little about religion. Everyone who knew him sensed immediately his religiosity, but not because of any affected piety.

Within a year of entering the school, Trevor had achieved legendary status. Rumors circulated, and some were confirmed, that he performed anonymous good deeds. In the course of a sustained and bitterly cold winter, classmates who rode the bus with him noted that instead of mittens or gloves, Trevor wore long white athletic socks—"tube" socks—over his hands. When asked about this, he would remove the socks sheepishly or, if he was outdoors, conceal them in his pockets. Asked directly why he wore socks on his hands instead of gloves, he answered, with a little laugh, "I just like them. They're warm."

But a friend from Trevor's neighborhood told another story. While tending to his sister, who boarded an earlier bus than Trevor's, he overheard one of her friends crying at the bus stop. When he asked the friend what was wrong, she said she had no mittens, and her hands were freezing. Trevor immediately gave the little girl his own down-filled gloves, a Christmas gift. "You can keep them" he told her. "They're a present."

Even more widely circulated was the story of the shoes. That same winter, on his way out of the school building one afternoon, Trevor stopped to see what was troubling a younger boy who was in a state of noisy agitation. It turned out that the boy had either lost a new pair of basketball shoes or else they had been stolen. The boy said his parents were going to "kill him" when they found out. The shoes he described were extravagantly elaborate, even a decade earlier costing nearly a hundred dollars. Moreover, the boy had lost another pair of athletic shoes the past fall, and his parents were still angry about that. Trevor told the boy the shoes would turn up. The despairing boy said, "I'll bet."

The next morning Trevor sought him out to ask if he had found his shoes. "No," was the morose reply. "I'll bet I never do. I didn't even have my name on them." Then, on a final hopeless note: "I can't even go to practice."

Later that day two inexplicable things happened. Trevor Diggs was called in to the dean because he had cut two classes. Trevor was apologetic but offered no explanation other than that he forgot to attend. "Were you distracted?" the dean asked. "I must have been," Trevor answered. He had never before missed a class, nor had he committed even a minor infraction of discipline. The second inexplicable thing was the appearance in the younger boy's locker of a box containing a new pair of basketball shoes. The shoes were not only the same brand name and highly specific type as the lost pair, they were the correct size.

The boy was incredulous, overjoyed, and he was as noisy about his find as he had been about his loss. The puzzle of the new shoes' appearance captured the imagination of the student body. Before long Trevor's name was advanced as the probable provider. The boy himself decided Trevor must have given him the new shoes: "He was the only one I really told, the only one who knew." When he asked Trevor directly, Trevor laughed and said he couldn't afford shoes like that even for himself, but, he said, "I'm glad you have them again."

In the minds of the students, the answer became clear-cut: Trevor bought the replacement shoes. I never heard a satisfactory explanation of where he would get so much money. I knew that neither he nor his aunt had money to spare. The telling point is that Trevor was perhaps the only boy in the school whom one could easily imagine making such a gesture. And the gestures continued. Most of them, like the gift of his gloves, were fairly straightforward. A boy who realized, at the last minute, that his after-school work detail conflicted with a family obligation would find, to his astonishment, that Trevor was cheerfully willing to man his vacuum cleaner for him. He was reliably willing to offer a welcoming word to scared new boys, succor to those devastated by bad college luck or cut from teams or passed over for leadership positions, parts in plays. He never ate lunch, but he carefully saved his food for others who might be late or especially hungry. In fact, his quiet, privately motivated benevolence probably took a toll on his academic achievement. Even before the phrase found a place in American jargon, Trevor was, in a school and out, "there for" everybody. He was not a bad student—and was by no means unintelligent. His output was really very difficult to assess. He did a little school work, extremely well.

It was easy to admire, and even to like, Trevor from a distance, to follow his progress as a boy-saint with amused detachment. And because I regarded him rather in this way, I was not prepared for a more significant encounter with him when it came.

Part of my job, when I became dean of students, was to hold students to basic standards of decorum: in dress, in their general conduct, in their manner of address. This included monitoring the school's traditional "senior speeches" so that nothing too hurtful or vulgar would be said from the stage. Historically the speeches have caused little trouble, the great majority being carefully composed and courteously received. But when Trevor was a senior, there was an ornery pocket of his classmates who pushed the guidelines for senior speeches to and past the limits. Due to spotty faculty supervision and a testy spirit of defiance on the part of a few boys, some utterly inappropriate talks were delivered. One of them rudely insulted a teacher's personal style—his dress, manner, taste. Another speaker, wearing a woman's tennis dress, said sexually suggestive things about the transsexual tennis player, Renée Richards.

In each of these cases it fell upon me to upbraid the boys, to inform their families that they had been offensive, and to impose certain disciplinary measures, including making another, more acceptable speech. On a number of counts, my actions were viewed angrily by the seniors and by many other students. There was talk of censorship and the denial of basic rights. Letters to the editor asked what made faculty standards—mine in particular—superior to student standards. Times were changing, it was said. Hadn't I ever seen *Saturday Night Live?* Why couldn't I take a joke?

At a point when I believed the resentment had run its course, yet another altogether unacceptable speech was given, a speech about the castration of bulls. Because I had gone so laboriously through the speech guidelines with the seniors after the previous lapses, I was less patient and more severe with the boy who spoke about bulls. Although he attempted a mild apology afterwards, he was far from contrite. In fact, he still seemed to be elated at the laughter he had evoked.

I sent him home. I told him he could not return until he had another, acceptable speech in hand and was prepared to apologize to the assembled school. The boy's parents called me at once to complain that I had responded excessively and unreasonably. I told them they were entitled to that opinion, but the decision stood. They asked me what had happened to my sense of humor. If I had been honest with them, I would have admitted to having lost all humor, all patience. I was sick of seniors and speeches and people asking me to adjust my ethical judgment in light of *Saturday Night Live.*

The boy was out of school two days writing another speech. In the course of his absence, criticism of my decision escalated wildly. Someone posted a survey on the library wall, inviting those who agreed or disagreed with my actions to sign their names on opposing columns. When I saw the survey, I was tempted to pull it down from the wall. No one had authorized or approved such a document. Angry and defensive as I was, I was also fascinated by the survey. By the end of the second day it was up, seemingly every student in the school had signed his name under the "disagree" heading. There was only one signature opposite: Trevor Diggs.

Later, when the speech incident was largely forgotten and student concerns had flown to other issues, I thanked Trevor for his support. And because I really wanted to know, I asked him if he believed that his classmate should have been sent home to write another speech. Trevor smiled in a way that expressed his discomfort with such a question. Then he said, "I felt bad for him being punished at home, but I felt even worse for you."

It would be hard for the students, and hard for me, to put into words the impact of Trevor's lone signature in the survey column. Because it was his, I felt more reassurance than I would have felt if half or even two thirds of the students had inscribed themselves on my side. And while I cannot claim it with certainty, I believe students saw something inspiring in Trevor's gesture too: that there was strength and even dignity in standing vulnerably alone.

Shortly after this conversation, Trevor was rushed to the hospital. An examination revealed he was on the brink of starvation, and his prospects for recovery were poor. But he did recover. Moreover, he recommitted himself to the therapy and group support prescribed for his chronic eating disorder. He graduated from the school, looking skeletal and beatific in his commencement suit.

He decided not to attend college but instead to enroll in a seminary. A year later he joined a monastic order, and I lost touch with him. Classmates believe he changed his name, possibly as a monastic requirement. I think about Trevor often. I hope that he has not grown thinner. I hope he has not, for his brothers' sake, effaced himself altogether.

DEAD BOYS

When little boys grow big enough to play in earnest, when they begin to thrust themselves into surrounding space, to try their speed, to see what can be made to roll, to roar, to burn, to explode, when they are at last left alone outdoors, beckoned by water and heights and culverts and caves—parents of necessity stop paying close attention. The truth of the matter is that boys passionate in their play are, like men passionate in their work, both inspiring and terrifying. The best of it is exhilarating, the worst of it unbearable. Some boys die, and many more come close.

Some boys die. They are by their nature at risk, acutely vulnerable. Some settings are safer than others, but none is really safe. The danger is in the boy, not in the neighborhood. The only reliable safeguard against the death of boys is not to conceive them.

Of course the death of a boy I have taught and known undoes me. But there is something distinctive in the aftermath, something like a hook or a message. Perhaps every boy teaches something, but the lessons of dead boys are especially vivid. One feature common to all such lessons is that death does not obliterate them. To the contrary, death fixes a boy's vitality at a single point and holds it there intact. It is not the dead boys but the living ones, the graduates, whose identities blur, who grow unrecognizably beefy and placid and old.

Seth Sampson will never grow old. He is forever a cherub and a clown and an acrobat. I met him when he was in the ninth grade and my student, a poor student then, in ancient history. Never before or since have I met a boy more pessimistic about his academic prospects. The very words, "O.K., take out a clean sheet of paper for a quiz," were enough to paralyze him. At first he would hand in nothing at all.

Working with him outside of class, I would ask him to read a passage of text and explain it to me. I feared the worst, but he surprised me. He could explain, once he got to know me, even very complex and sophisticated material. One day after school in my office I asked him to read a chapter of our ancient Rome text. When he finished, I asked him several pointed questions on its key points. He answered them all clearly and thoroughly. Then I said, "O.K., Seth, I am going to ask you these same questions again, only this time it counts." He stiffened. "What do you mean 'it counts'?" I told him it meant it counted for a grade, that I would grade his answers just as if they were a test. This threw Seth into a muddle, and he was unable to make sense of anything in the chapter.

The following afternoon I had Seth in again and asked him to read the next chapter of the text. "Is it going to count?" he asked. Absolutely not, I told him. He read, and again he revealed a good understanding when we discussed the material afterward. Because we had done so before with no productive effect, I did not bother to point out again that he obviously had the ability to excel in history, that he somehow had to get over his "test" panic. Instead, I took out my grade book and gave him an A on what I decided on the spot was equivalent of a "half test." When Seth reminded me that I said it wasn't going "to count," I told him I had changed my mind. Why shouldn't it count, I asked him; he obviously understood the material.

By assuring Seth repeatedly that, in his case, nothing counted in history, he began doing a little better. He would now answer factual questions, but he would only write tentative little essays, when fully developed ones were required. This turned out to be a far greater challenge than getting him over his test panic. I tried requiring him to fill out a specified number of pages in his exam book, even if he had nothing to say. At first he was unable to do this, even by repeating himself. In time his essays grew longer, but they never contained more than a simple point or two, never approaching what was expected.

Unsure myself whether Seth was genuinely limited or whether he was somehow "blocked," I tried another trick. I called him in after he had written a typically insubstantial exam and I told him that I thought he had made a breakthrough this time, that he had made some solid points and was beginning to get the hang of writing essays. I gave him a higher grade, a C or C +, than he had gotten on a history test all year. He regarded me warily.

His next test was, if anything, worse than the previous one. I was tempted to abandon my gimmick, but instead decided to give it one more try. No one in the class did particularly well on the exam. There were only a few Bs, and the rest of the grades were lower. I gave Seth one of the Bs. "Definitely a breakthrough," I wrote on his test book. This time, for some reason, he believed me. Slowly, gratifyingly, fact, example, thesis, and extended reflection began to appear in Seth's written work. He became before my eyes a good, an original, a self-directed student of history.

Better than that, a much more energetic, more surprising boy came to life in the school. Seth Sampson turned out to be a phenomenal clown. He had a highly developed athleticism which did not count for much in school sports, except in the annual gymnastics exhibition. Seth could walk on his hands, execute one-armed push-ups, juggle, tumble, and dive. Inspired by the movie comic Chevy Chase, Seth mastered the art of falling down spectacularly. He could trip himself and fall down forwards or backwards in a way that left no doubt that he had broken bones. The school has a wide central staircase broken by two large, carpeted landings. Seth's *tour de force* was losing his footing on the top stair and tumbling head-over-heels, arms akimbo down the stairs, across both landings, to the bottom. He was never hurt.

He loved to fall; that is, he loved the art of seeming to fall. What he loved was the surprise and the delight. His emergence as a scholar, as a comic sprite, and as a wonderfully generous soul around school seemed almost part of a plan to surprise us. He would pitch in for any kind of service project or school clean-up. If the alumni office staff found themselves short-handed for a big mailing, Seth would volunteer to stuff envelopes after school until he was late for dinner. He was the only boy known to climb the school flag pole. He was rumored to have sneaked onto the school roof at night, pried open a skylight over the pool, and dropped forty feet into the diving well. It was hard to be cautionary or disapproving when Seth toppled or tumbled. I remember feeling once, when he had righted himself at the bottom of the stairs after a spectacular fall, that he was as beamingly happy a boy as I had ever seen.

A year and a day after Seth Sampson graduated from the school, he died. He had completed a successful freshman college year and came home to see some younger boys graduate. When he and his friends drove back to the college campus to retrieve their belongings, they found their dormitory locked. This did not faze Seth. Once before he had entered the building when it had been locked. He lived in a dormered room on the top floor. By holding on to a drain pipe he hoisted himself up from window ledge to window ledge until he reached the roof — which he did to the cheers of his friends on the ground. Balancing like a tightrope walker, arms outstretched, Seth made his way across a patch of slate roof to reach the dormer window of his own room. This, he had assured his friends, was the easy part. And at that moment it began to rain.

The pitched slate became slippery as ice. His horrified friends then witnessed the unthinkable: Seth falling four floors onto the grass below. The sight and sound of it were sickening. Seth lay in a heap before them, then he rose wide-eyed to his feet. He said he was O.K., then he lay back down again. A friend ran to a phone to call an ambulance. But help arrived too late. The nerves activating his lungs had been severed. No one could clearly explain how, before he died, he had arisen and spoken. Seth loved to fall; that is, he loved the art of seeming to fall. What he loved was the surprise and the delight.

* * *

Tom Truro was a boy who seemed only partially to exist. I say this because all of his encounters with me and, so far as I could tell, with anybody else, were so hurried and so oblique that it was difficult to assess what actually transpired. Although in no way antagonistic, Tom looked away when he spoke, seemingly in a hurry to get onto something else. When he talked at any length, his speech became almost inaudible. Mainly he communicated in stacatto single syllables — in *yeahs* and *rights* and a peculiar little sigh that he would cut short by inhaling it back into himself.

His classmates contracted his name to "Tonto." The nickname made more than just aural sense. The Lone Ranger's Tonto suggested less a person than a shadowy double of a person, an aura, a shade. The

Indian Tonto wasn't really around much, and neither was Tom Truro. Where Tom went and what he actually did with his time were never clear to me.

Tom's mother and father were both criminal attorneys, and they had built a considerable reputation in the city for winning innocent verdicts or mild sentences for defendants made out by the press to be hopelessly guilty. The Truros were said to be ruthless, to bully prosecutors and witnesses alike. I never saw this side of Tom's parents, who came in to school fairly frequently to be apprised of Tom's chronic troubles: truancy and slack academic performance. The Truros took pains to explain how busy they were, how seldom home, how unable to look after a flaky teenager. "You know," Mr. Truro said once, "the kid has everything he could ask for, even a woman to keep house for him and to cook his meals." Intrigued by this housekeeping/cooking arrangement, I inquired further and was told that Tom and his family never ate meals together. Never? I asked. Never, they said, absolutely never, and Tom later confirmed this. He either took his meals out or ate what was left for him by Anetta, a woman employed by his parents. Tom was at this time sixteen.

In addition to passing days at a time without a glimpse of either parent, Tom had no friends—that is, no person he called a friend or who called him friend. There were people, both boys and girls, he would see, but no one he said he wanted to hang around with. When Tom telephoned or drove to a classmate's house to "see" him, it was always to ask a specific question, to drop something off or to pick something up. When I pressed him about being so constantly alone, Tom, looking past me, would say something like, "No. No way. That's the way I like things." A stifled sigh, and he would be out the door.

Tom's troubles at school mounted, not because he acted out unpleasantly, but because he was so seldom there and therefore in scholastic arrears. He had picked out, and his parents had paid for, a high-performance sports car, a Porsche, and the word among the students was that Tom spent his days behind the wheel, driving murderously fast. It became clear that he was not meeting his commitments at school, and his parents saw no way to intervene effectively. So he was sent to military boarding school.

Tom agreed to apply on the condition that if he did well academically for a year, he could come back home. At the year's end, he reapplied to us. It was not easy to judge how well he had done at the military school. His transcript was very complicated. He had begun and dropped many courses due, he explained, to "incorrect placement." There were no distinctly low marks. His instructors' comments were not unfavorable, but they were highly general; I couldn't really locate Tom in his reapplication materials.

In truth, I had no faith that I would ever locate Tom Truro, hold him still, pin him down. Except that he had grown bigger and more rangy, he was unchanged. He was as elusive as ever. I remember feeling that I now understood the literary expression "absently," as in "he stared absently at his companion." While he was away Tom had grown deeply absent. It is hard to explain, and I believe it reflects badly on me in my post at the time, but it seemed that as Tom continued to miss school, it somehow mattered less: that Tom mattered less. This was of course an appalling, morally unacceptable response, but Tom's encounters with us had grown so glancing that he sometimes seemed no more substantial than a bit of typescript on an absentee report. In the course of several interviews after he returned, I felt only once that I was in the presence of a fully dimensional person, and then just briefly. He had, he told me with some force, a new car. I have forgotten the make, only that Tom called it "a real racing machine."

One evening shortly afterward, at what would have been the dinner hour, Tom raced this machine into oblivion: up over a guard rail, airborne over a steep ravine, then broken over rock and water. Someone from the Truros' firm, but not the Truros, called to tell me about the death and the services to follow.

The service was nonreligious and very short — in a way as oblique as Tom himself. A eulogy lacking specific reference or incident made a kind of case for Tom as a romantic quester. I could not think of Tom on a quest, speeding through the twilight in his sinister black car. I could think of him only as veering away from me, from everybody. Nothing there, he may have felt — at least not enough.

Somebody had taped onto his coffin a sheet of paper bearing the slogan "Ride like the wind, Tonto." I started when I saw it. For a moment I was angry at what seemed to be such vulgar sentimentality. But the slogan also struck something deep. Again, it had nothing to do with the romantic image of a solitary horseman speeding through the night; what struck me was "like the wind." Like the wind. That was Tom, starved in a way, detaching himself from human encumbrance, the myth of family, the claptrap routine of school. I could see Tom veering away from all that, no more than wind.

* * *

Ricky Wise's mother told me he was gravely ill when I went to visit him in his intensive-care unit. As it happened, he died about an hour after I left his room. But even before I heard the finality of that news, I knew that my understanding of the human "life span" had been altered forever.

In the last hour of his life, Ricky Wise held court. He was fifteen years old, the youngest person in the room, mortally ill, but a Vesuvius of vitality. He had summoned his parents, his older sister, a friend of hers whom he liked, and two of his teachers, including me. His grandmother was waiting outside, but Ricky did not want to see her. She was notorious for her platitudes, and Ricky could not stand that or, for the moment, her, and he said so pointedly. Neither of his parents felt compelled to correct him.

Ricky's stomach cancer had been diagnosed the previous autumn. A massive malignancy was removed, and his prospects were promising because of his youth and strength. But the cancer persisted, spread the length of his digestive tract from his throat to his bowel, and was ultimately inoperable. That final afternoon the disease had effectively severed his throat from his esophagus. He could maintain enough moisture in his mouth to speak only by sucking on finely crushed ice. He was glad to see us.

He talked lucidly and well, but he grew painfully agitated if he was interrupted. He made it clear that he needed to say what he was saying. He did not care at all if he was agreeable—he spoke disagreeably about a number of matters, including his grandmother. He needed to be completely honest, and while these were not his words, he seemed to want to establish a kind of closure on his life, to express its coherence as a story.

"I'm a materialist," he said to my surprise, "And materialism is right. It doesn't matter if some people have more, provided they use it to make beautiful things. Like a beautiful house." Even before his illness, Ricky took a precocious interest in great houses: suburban mansions and country estates. He was the only freshman in the school who pored over *Architectural Digest, Connoisseur,* and *Town and Country* in the hope of seeing elegant rooms. "As long as it's beautiful, it doesn't matter who runs it, but someone has to do it, someone has to keep the beauty going."

"The best thing that happened to me," he said, "is beautiful houses—just seeing them, knowing they are there. Traveling," he added, "is also good."

Ricky closed his eyes and was, I thought, sleeping when he said, "I'm so lucky." No one knew how to respond to this.

"I know I'm not lucky because I'm going to die. I'm going to miss a lot. I'm never going to get married, and I'm never going to see how everything turns out. But as soon as I realized I was going to die, that I would die for sure, it was also a tremendous relief. I don't ever have to worry about anything again. I don't have to worry about college, I don't have to worry about a job—about anything. And that's amazing." He made this point so convincingly that, in truth, it was hard not to envy him his liberation from responsibility.

Ricky's eyes rolled back, then closed. Again I thought we had lost him to sleep, but in a minute he was blinking his way back into our midst. "That's the morphine," he said. "It just takes you with it."

"Did I tell you," he said with new strength, "how smart I feel? Over the past few days I have moments when I think I've figured out everything, how everything fits together. It's such a relief when that happens. Really!"

My final memory of Ricky is his pleasure in being relieved from care, his pleasure in his new perspective, his wisdom. "Do you know how old I feel?" he asked, smiling, eyes closed again.

"How old?" I asked.

"I feel so old," he said, "and so smart. I feel like I'm eighty."

And then he slept.

* * *

When a boy dies, when he disappears suddenly from your midst, you can find yourself (strange to say) wondering if he was ever fully there. The part of him you knew is of course missing, but there was so much—most of him, really—that was never available to you. Is there a possibility that boys are never wholly in this world? Are they, or perhaps only certain aspects of them, on a kind of spiritual loan, recallable without warning?

My colleagues and I lost a boy, Jacob Hummer, to suicide. More to reassure ourselves than anything else, we compose stronger and stronger explanations for why he did it. Coming to this kind of understanding, however, leaves the greater mystery intact: who was this extraordinary boy who made such a violent exit?

Jake Hummer was very rugged and very gentle. Even in kindergarten he was circumspect and considerate, easy to defer to. As a little boy he was seraphically cute; with his wide grey eyes, fair skin, finely chiseled features, and tumble of curls, he could have been an attendant angel in a composition by Verrocchio or Leonardo. When he stretched out into adolescent leanness, his face grew longer, and his jawline set in a way that made him look very determined, but the curls persisted, creating an impression of exuberance that he possibly did not feel.

By the time he was in junior high school it was understood by his classmates and teachers that Jake Hummer would excel in anything he took up. With very little foot speed, he became an outstanding athlete: good hands, good balance, good judgment, and surprising strength. He had a gift for judging balls in the air — for catching and intercepting passes, for getting the jump on a long fly ball in the outfield. He became a talented varsity athlete, a quiet competitor, a captain.

He was also a quick, deep, retentive scholar. He was not effusive in class, but he was not withdrawn either. His written work was surprisingly acute and sophisticated. It was as if the writing circuits in his brain stored more words, connected them more subtly and imaginatively than his speaking circuits did. In the higher maths, too, and in chemistry and physics, he was a deft and intuitive problem-solver. He worked steadily and reliably, but he did not appear to stretch or hurry himself, and he never complained about the amount of work he was asked to do. He always earned high honors, was inducted into the highly selective Cum Laude Society, and his name was usually third or fourth, never first or second, in the scholastic ranking of his class.

After he died, some of his friends told me that the only way to know Jake Hummer was to know him out of doors. He was, whenever school schedules allowed, an outdoorsman: a backpacker, hiker, climber, spelunker. He liked especially to be on the water, to be alone on the water, at best in a shell or a canoe on a remote Canadian lake. Even when he was at home he liked to lie out in a sleeping bag in the middle of his suburban back yard under the stars. One summer, when his family were nearing the end of a stay in their cabin in northern Ontario, Jake surprised his father by stating, with special force, that there had to be a way to live this cabin, lake, and pine-forest life year-round.

For my own part, I don't believe it was possible to know Jake without knowing his deep immersion in music. He was a superb guitar player. He responded immediately to the first acoustic guitar playing he heard as a child—blue grass music and folk tunes—and quickly learned to produce those tinkling syncopations himself. There were lessons at first, but by the time he was a teenager he had staked out his own, highly personal course of musical development: listening, imitating, embellishing. His ear was true, and he played so clearly that he made even a standard blues or ragtime tune sound almost classical in its precision. Somehow, with all of his other commitments and diversions, he managed to play the guitar for solitary hours on end, often late into the night.

Jake preferred playing to himself, alone, but he was too appealingly good — and too compliant — to avoid audiences altogether. Other friends who played and sang included him in ensembles, some of them bearing hip-nonsensical names, and their performances at private parties and school social events were warmly received.

Despite his talent, Jake was an unlikely celebrity. He neither flaunted his playing nor did he seek out opportunities to play in public. But when he did perform, he was compelling to watch. He did not announce any of the group's songs, and he never sang, except for an occasional, muted back-up line. He never looked out into the audience; he kept his gaze fixed intently on the strings of his guitar. Whether seated on a stool or standing up, he looked entirely comfortable in his absorption.

In the spring of Jake's junior year, the school's arts association planned a rather loosely structured Saturday afternoon musicale: The Outer Valley Sunshine Festival. Student folk singers, guitar players, rock groups, and comedians were invited to perform. A courtyard bordering the school pond and woods was chosen. Amplifiers, mixers, and microphones were hired for the afternoon. The affair was to be (and was) emphatically casual. Anybody who wanted to could play. There were no rehearsals. "Make music if you feel like it," the posters said. "Listen to music if you feel like it." A half dozen grills were set up to cook hot dogs and hamburgers. Soft drinks and fruit juice were provided at cost. An admission fee of a dollar was asked to cover expenses, and students were "on their honor" to pay it, as the outdoor site offered easy access from all sides.

The appointed afternoon turned out to be lovely: a prematurely warm, breezy spring day. There was sun, but soft sun, creating a gauzy quality to the atmosphere. There were more buds than leaves, and the new grass in the courtyard smelled positively sweet.

The arts association succeeded: they had staged a free and easy, radically non-scholastic experience. There was an agreeable hint of charcoal smoke in the air, stirring breezes, bird song, and the unhurried arcs of frisbees overhead. The boys and girls wore jeans and tee shirts as vividly colored as flags. The soft air seemed to diffuse the periodic wailing and growling of the rock players, and the other guitarists were as gentle as wind chimes. In all, quite a crowd turned out. Never before in my experience at the school had students created so restful an occasion.

No one wanted it to end at the scheduled hour. And as it happened, the most accomplished act—Jake Hummer and his friends—had not performed yet. Permission was sought and given to keep the festival going for a while. Parents arriving to pick up sons and daughters joined the crowd. Baseball players, returning from a long double-header, their white uniforms tinted yellow by late afternoon sun, drifted into the gathering. Something was said over the p.a., and Jake and his friends began to play.

They played and sang James Taylor's sad ballads, songs about needing a friend, and hoping love and honesty would be enough to see a troubled soul through another day. There was a slow, surprisingly tuneful version of "Blue Suede Shoes." They played a number of folk tunes, elegant treble harmonies picked out over full-bodied progressions of chords below. The boys' metal finger picks scraped a little on the steel strings, so that there was a slightly hoarse tone to what otherwise could have been a wonderfully robust, syncopated music box.

The tunes pressed forward to their resolutions, and the ripe and darkening afternoon proceeded toward nightfall, but there was at the same time a stillness. I am sure that I was not alone in sensing holiness in the concluding moments of the Outer Valley Sunshine Festival. If memory serves, Jake Hummer was playing then, by himself. He was seated upon a stool, hunched over the body of his guitar, as if in rapt, silent dialogue with his own gently jingling creation.

Jake went to Harvard University, but left after the first year to make music with a band. The group played college campuses, then was booked into some popular clubs. For a while Jake's band toured as an opening act for a rising rock group. After about a year of playing professionally, Jake's friends cut a limited-edition record they hoped would get the attention of the recording industry. I heard it and thought its country-rock sound was very polished, even a little slick. While the quality of the recording was undeniable, I couldn't hear Jake in it.

Shortly after I heard the record, I learned that Jake was no longer in the group. There had been a falling out or he was sick. His parents told me later that he had sunk into a kind of depression, a breakdown. He could no longer play in front of an audience; his fingers froze. He did not believe he could manage returning to college, nor could he bring himself to do anything else. He went home to his parents' house and secluded himself. Therapists were consulted, medicine prescribed. It was determined that, in the course of the band's touring and club dates, Jake had taken to smoking pot. At home he kept to his old room, chain smoking. He slept most of the day and ate irregularly, mainly junk food. For a time he took to reading classic texts in philosophy: Plato, Aristotle, Hobbes, Locke, Rousseau. Then this stopped too.

Alienated—I am sure he believed forever—from the campus routines and working lives of his former classmates and friends, he spoke only to members of his family, but not easily and not often. He no longer played music or listened to it.

Jake Hummer's depression communicated to his family a terrible, enveloping certainty that he was finished. So quiet in its manifestations, his misery was a palpable presence in the house, infectious, too dreadful to name. The family endured a period of aggravated waiting. Afterward, a physician close to the Hummers wrote them a warm letter saying that, in his experience of patients of all ages, infants through geriatrics, he was increasingly sure there was a unique life span implanted, perhaps genetically, in each person. This deep, hidden program unfolds independently of environmental conditions and expectations. And though some infants fail to thrive and some elderly men and women thrive for decades without apparent physiological means, there is in everyone a powerful inner knowledge of the allotted span. Jake's span, the physician suggested, may have been twenty-two years. And while such an abbreviated script may seem unfair and even tragic, there was, in this doctor's view, an intensity to the experience of shorter spans that gave them every bit of the depth and richness of longer ones. Jake may have been, as the Hindus say, a very old soul at twenty-two. Moreover, the doctor suggested, Jake almost certainly knew it, knew it in the center of his being.

The end itself was deafening, unthinkable. Alone in his room one airless afternoon Jake somehow managed to depress the trigger of a shotgun while the barrel was at his chest. His mother ran to see. Shock, of course, is the right word for her response, but at the very core of shock, and in a way defining it, is its opposite: confirmation. A wordless, electrically charged No! will intermittently rise to that woman's consciousness as long as she lives. But there is also, consciously or not, an acknowledging Yes!

The loud, ringing moment of Jake Hummer's negation is passed. I was not a witness, but I have imagined the scene. My musing does not linger there; it proceeds instead to another frozen moment, this one alive. It is near the end of the Outer Valley Sunshine Festival, and Jake is sitting on his stool, comfortably cradling his guitar, coaxing a jingling melody into the air. It is first spring, and the afternoon light is soft with haze. The melody is all around Jake's head, like some playful extension of his curls. It is so good, and he is so happily preoccupied, I find myself wanting a private, timeless place like that of my own.

INSPIRING BOYS

Teaching boys is hard. It is physically and emotionally draining. The pay in even the most prosperous schools is worrisomely low. Every demonstrably good teacher I have known has possessed personal gifts that would translate profitably into other lines of work. Salary does not keep committed teachers in the profession; nor, in my opinion, does any abstract principle, such as "the need for an educated citizenry." Men and women give their lives to teaching because they take genuine pleasure in the company of children, specifically children engaged in directed, purposeful activity, children who will before one's eyes achieve new understanding, appreciation, mastery. Children of course do not strive ceaselessly and reverently after these things. But nearly every child can be seen to strive sometimes, and a few strive so passionately they defy explanation. It is this striving, this trusting susceptibility to inspiration that inspires—and not merely pleases—teachers. Inspiring boys have periodically transformed my school. The inspiring boys I have known constitute the only continuing education I have had.

Seth Levin was a ninth grader when I met him. He was small and slight, cheerful, and enormously intelligent—the uncontested top scholar in his class. His father founded a business which bottled sparkling water, and it continues to prosper wildly. Seth is a deeply pious Jew, and there was something pious, something passionate about his dedication to school tasks. By passionate, I do not mean obsessive or compulsive. In algebra, in biology, in my ancient history class, he was not a fact-monger (although he was phenomenally retentive and precise), and he never asked after a grade (his were uniformly high). He hungered after the point of things. If we were reading about the trial and death of Socrates, he endured the discussion of the facts and circumstances with a helpful patience. But during the discussion of whether surrendering one's life for a principle was justifiable, Seth came to life. Of course it was! he would almost cry out. Even saving your life is a principle. The real issue, Seth maintained, is *which* principle should prevail. Seth was enchanted by Socrates' speculations about the possibility of an after-life. I remember his arguing—and winning—the point that Socrates' almost lighthearted response to his death sentence was not just one of his personality traits, but rather the logical result of believing the truth is objective and real; if the source of everything valuable and real exists independently of your own bodily biology, then bodily biology is of no great importance. Your living body, Seth explained, is a means to experiencing what is true; mistaking your own life for the truth itself is an understandable mistake, but still a mistake. For a while, when and after he said it, we all saw it.

When Seth had his hand up or when he was writing furiously in his exam booklet, you could actually feel him trying. Without even knowing it, Seth's effort was contagious. It was hard to teach an under-productive class if Seth was in it. Nowhere was his effort more apparent than in those areas of school life in which he did not excel. Small, thin, and not espe-cially coordinated physically, Seth worked out strenu-ously in the school's physical education program. More willing than able, he was frequently injured in the course of exerting himself in informal sports. Tradi-tionally, the school is an athletic powerhouse; it would have been unthinkable for Seth not to embrace a value so obviously important to the community. Seth be-came a devoted, even a fairly loud, fan. He took up sports writing for the school paper, struggling as ear-nestly with the idiom as he might with a foreign lan-guage. I still have the paper in which his first sports article appeared. The lead ran as follows: "Garnering a packet of key dual wins, the J.V. spikemen, featuring a bevy of strong-running frosh, strode lightly past rev-ered opponents from neighboring Beachwood and Highland Heights."

In late winter my classes were studying the Mid-dle Ages, and I thought I might convey a sense of monasticism—specifically, the rule of St. Benedict of Nursia—by practicing it for a class-length period. I required everyone to spend forty-five minutes as if it were the monks' hour of Compline, during which only intellectual work or prayer was allowed. No one could speak. Idleness was a sin.

To a background of taped plainsong, the ninth graders sat in a partially darkened classroom, attempt-ing either to pray or to study. At the end of the class, I told the boys I had been able to concentrate on the work before me only about thirty of the forty-two minutes allotted. Some of the students, mainly those who prayed, said they did better than that. Seth supposed he had been busy for forty minutes.

I was once in the administrative offices after school, checking my mail. Seth was there, asking a secretary when the next bus would leave the school. "In an hour," she replied. Seth's face fell. He looked at his large, complicated watch, thought for a minute, and asked the secretary if there was anything that needed to be done around the office. As it happened, it was the end of a marking period, and an extensive mailing to parents had to be collated and stuffed into envelopes. Seth stayed and did it, chatting amiably, a sharp eye on the work of his flying hands.

* * *

Like Seth Levin, Edward Lee was a brilliant scholar, one of the most talented young mathematicians in the United States, although I did not know this when I first encountered him at school. A slightly bemused, squinting, thoroughly lost boy, he approached me on New Student Orientation Day and asked me a question which I at first misunderstood: "Could you please tell me where I belong?" The courtesy and calmness of his manner suggested, just for a second, a higher, rather than a lost, being.

Another early impression of Edward was equally unprofessional. He was Korean, and he had an oddly elongated face. The line of his eyes was drawn so tightly that he seemed always to be straining to see. At first glance, he looked prematurely old, a little wizened. His mother, by contrast, looked young and was very beautiful. I wondered, and I know I speculated out loud, how such a beautiful woman could produce so homely a son. But as is so often the case in school, actual experience presents more heavy-handed lessons than any morality play; Edward Lee became beautiful before my eyes.

I have never had a better student than Edward Lee; that is, I have never learned more from a student. He wrote eloquently. In fact, it seemed to me, he wrote perfectly, although I faulted him sometimes for writing so little on what I thought were vast, rich topics. He once asked me, "How would I say more?" Although he must have asserted many things in the time I spent with him in and outside the classroom, I can only remember questions.

He was a member of a very bright and fiercely opinionated class—Introduction to Philosophy—my class. One afternoon, argument was raging, not very productively, over the relationship between ethical prescriptions and faith in the *Sermon on the Mount*. How did a maxim like "turn the other cheek" or "consider the lilies" or even "do unto others" derive from a requirement of faith: "Our Father . . . hallowed be thy name." Is the *Sermon on the Mount* saying, one irritated boy asked, that you can only do good things if you acknowledge God—or is it saying that by doing good things you acknowledge God? Something crudely like a faith-versus-works discussion was escalating noisily when I noted Edward's uninsistent raised hand.

"Why are you linking the two things at all?" he asked.

"They're linked in the Bible."

Edward persisted: "They are both discussed, but are they linked? I see references to acknowledging God but not doing good things, and references to doing good things but not acknowledging God. Aren't they separate, different things?"

"But what would God think of good deeds from someone who didn't believe in God?"

"Wouldn't God know they were good?" Edward asked.

"But that's assuming there is a God!" someone blurted out. "Assume there is no God. Aren't good deeds just as good without a God?"

Edward smiled. "I personally think they would be, but does that matter as much as God thinking they were good?"

Until Edward Lee said that, I had not really understood that the subject of the very course I was teaching was: What makes things matter?

Edward Lee was incisive, naturally analytic, brilliant. He was warm-hearted, but not really light-hearted. He was not much like a boy, and I believe this saddened him. Perhaps sensing this, Colin Blount, an irreverent and very eccentric colleague of mine set himself to locating Edward's lighter side.

Colin looked after the after-school soccer program for boys who elected to play that sport but who were not interested or skilled enough to play on an inter-scholastic team. These "general soccer" boys met on bracing, sometimes chilly afternoons on the most marginal fields. "Captains" and sides were chosen each session, and there was some energy, but little intensity, in their anarchic pursuit of the ball over the scuffed turf.

When the number of boys showing up made uneven sides, Colin, although nearly fifty and fairly broad of paunch, liked to play for whoever was undermanned, officiating with his whistle as he ambled along with the boys.

Edward Lee was a "general soccer" player, usually taciturn and minimally engaged. One October afternoon when his whistle ended the games, Colin beckoned Edward to his side and asked that he stick around for a while. They had both "played" defense that afternoon, but the action had taken place almost entirely at the offensive end of the field. There was something Colin thought Edward should learn.

Whatever Edward was thinking I can only guess, since I only heard Colin's account of the encounter. Apparently Colin spent the next half hour in the brisk air of the deserted athletic fields teaching Edward Lee an old vaudeville routine. "It'll pass the time the next time we're on defense," Colin said hastily.

"Is it required?" Edward reportedly said.

"Absolutely!" said the swollen-gutted man with the whistle. "Change your whole outlook. Change your life!"

Then they set about it. First the words to a little ditty, then some mincing dance steps while leaning over imaginary canes. When I actually witnessed the routine later, I was stunned. Colin would bellow, and

Edward would answer in a deadpan monotone, but right on cadence:

Colin: Say, Mr. Lee!
Edward: Yes, Mr. Blount?
Colin: Say, Mr. Lee!
Edward: Yes, Mr. Blount?
Both: We're the sweetest soccer team in all the world . . .
Colin: On the defense, you and me.
Edward: That's Mr. Blount!
Colin: And Mr. Lee . . .
Edward: Positively, Mr. Blount
Colin: And absolutely, Mr. Lee!

Then off Colin would go into a second identical verse, perhaps raising and shaking an imaginary topper from his head. By this time, Edward would have stopped, regarding Colin impassively, as if awaiting further instructions. The whole business, or even thinking about it, made Colin shriek with laughter.

For reasons I'm not sure I fully understand, I came genuinely to like the routine. When I saw them approaching one another from opposite ends of a crowded corridor or meeting on the school's central staircase after lunch, I was always elated to hear Colin's

Say, Mr. Lee!

and the beat-perfect response

Yes, Mr. Blount?

Again, this little improvisation gave me great pleasure. I might have been tempted to say its appeal lay in the goofy incongruity of Colin and Edward together, or of Edward and vaudeville. But that would not quite cover it. The incongruity made it funny, but it was something else, a deep congruity that struck the responsive chord. One day, I hailed Edward on his way out of my philosophy class. "Say, Mr. Lee!" I said. He gave me a little smile. I told him I got a big kick out of his routine with Mr. Blount. His smile broadened. "Yes," he said. "Do you think he's pleased?"

* * *

Tony Alvarez was not the kind of boy, at least while he was in school, who thought much about pleasing people. Tony was the fourth boy and sixth of eleven children in the Alvarez family. His father groomed horses, and his mother, a wildly unkempt and pretty woman, ran on the Democratic ticket for various local offices, without much success. The Alvarezes lived on the semi-rural outskirts of the city. They had little money and few comforts.

Mrs. Alvarez brought Tony to school to interview and to apply because, as she said, "I think we've got something here." She did indeed have something. Tony's aptitude testing was extremely high. He also had enthusiastic praise from the teachers in his local school, one of whom wrote, "You just can't hold him back." He was admissible and deserving of financial aid on a number of counts, but what sold me was the force of enthusiasm he expressed in his interview.

"What are your special interests?" he was asked.

"I'm interested in everything. There isn't anything I'm not interested in. I like reading. I like reading Dickens. I like everything to do with language. I like science. I like entomology . . ."

"You like insects?" A member of the biology faculty asked.

Tony's face clouded. "I'm not too crazy about insects."

The biology teacher explained that he assumed liking entomology, the study of insects, meant that he would like insects.

"Oh, no," Tony said. "What I meant was I like to study where words come from, what goes into a word like 'altitude' or 'restaurant'."

"You mean etymology," I said. "That's the study of words."

"That's it," said Tony, and then he laughed. "Insects! I didn't know what you were getting at. What's the right word?"

"Etymology, e-t-y-m-o-l-o-g-y."

"Etymology," Tony said. "Thank you. Thank you very much. I hate not knowing the right thing."

Tony did hate it, and it made him, in addition to stimulating company, a frequent pain in the neck; he was a little like Huck Finn with a very high I.Q. His questions and challenges to those who gave him unsatisfying answers grew increasingly sharp as he progressed through the school. Why did students have to pay a full year's lunch fee if they chose not to eat the prepared lunches? Because, I told him, we hire a kitchen staff and order food under the assumption that a certain number will have to be fed each day. If we let the amount of money coming in vary with what kids felt like eating each day, we would have to lay off staff on some days, hire them back on others. Also, we couldn't plan how much to order, if students decided daily what they wanted to eat or if they would eat.

"That's not the way a free economy works." Tony told me.

"It's the way our kitchen works," I told Tony. "And I'll bet it's the way your kitchen works at home."

"I'll bet it isn't. First, we don't pay for meals at home. Secondly, we don't all eat the same thing. My mom tries to give us what we like. Sometimes we have a lot of different things for supper. If people don't like what's served, they don't have to eat it. And they certainly don't have to pay if they don't eat it."

"By the way, Tony," I said to him, warming, "You don't pay for your lunches here, either."

A mistake. Bad judgment. Tony grew furious: "So what? What's that got to do with the issue we were discussing?"

Why, Tony wondered over the course of his junior and senior years, were students required to attend classes? Wasn't the loss theirs if they missed something important? Nothing is required at college. What kind of practice for college life were required classes, required assemblies, required lunches, required service? What was the moral value of serving the community if it was required? Not voluntary. Involuntary. What was the point of a dress code? What was the esthetic or moral difference between denim (not allowed) and khaki (allowed), basketball shoes (not allowed) and boating shoes (allowed)? If smoking was forbidden because it was harmful, why did faculty continue to smoke? If faculty were given coffee, why weren't students given coffee? Who paid for the faculty coffee? Did any student tuition go for faculty coffee? If not, how was the coffee paid for? Why were heavily committed, interesting younger teachers paid less than clock-watching, boring older teachers?

Tony wanted answers to these and dozens of other questions. Incomplete answers, logically inconsistent answers, any answers given on authority served only to kindle additional, more ferocious challenges to the status quo. Told once, directly and forcefully, "Tony, you are a real pain in the ass," he answered, "What kind of an answer is that? If you asked me a question, and I said 'Mr. Lindholm, you are a real pain in the ass,' what would you do?"

In retrospect, I believe Tony's sheer industry saved him from being a "real pain in the ass." He grew his hair irritatingly long, his clothes were only technically within the dress code, he loudly challenged seemingly every disciplinary decision, new policy, building proposal. He was nosey about school finances, faculty politics, even faculty personal lives. But he took great, infectious pleasure in work. He was a voracious reader, a writer of long, rich, sloppily composed papers. He was a vigorous, tireless debater, a bull-dog of a running back, an overly ambitious but nonetheless inspired designer of independent science projects. Outwardly and superficially an angry young man, a rebel, he was lovingly devoted to his friends and to those few teachers who would argue, listen, and laugh with him long into darkening afternoons. He was a dutiful son and brother, especially to his three baby sisters, to whom he was something of a father, staying home to watch them nearly every weekend of his high school life. Tony thoroughly disapproved of drugs and drinking, and he could not abide the idea of rich people wasting time.

Some of his friends were from well-to-do families, and Tony chided them relentlessly about their comforts and privileges. I had heard him opine so stridently on the subject of "rich people" and "country club people" that I wondered if he wasn't falling reflexively into reverse snobbery. I resolved to talk to him about it, but when an opportunity arose, Tony unloosed a torrent of his own concerns.

He had just returned from a spring vacation to Florida, where he had been a guest of a friend's family for two weeks. "David's practically my best friend," Tony said, "but that family is in real trouble." The trouble, according to Tony, was that the family's activities, kids' and parents' both, were organized around spending money. "Here we were on this incredible beach, right on the ocean. We could swim, ride the waves until we dropped. There was every kind of sea shell in the world—shells they sell in stores up here— right on the beach. There was every kind of bird you could imagine. The idea that there really are birds like pelicans blew my mind. I stood right next to one, a foot away. But all David's brothers wanted to do was go to town. Go to the store! They wanted everything they saw. If another kid had a special life jacket or some funny kind of goggles, they had to have them right away. They kept digging and whining for things. They wanted videos for the VCR every second they were in the house. They wanted new Nintendo games. They wanted to pick up in Florida right where they left off in Cleveland. They made their parents buy them every-thing anybody was selling to eat—ice cream, hot dogs, fries, soda. It didn't matter that they had tons of the same stuff in the fridge at home or even in their own picnic basket. If it was for sale, they had to have it right then. Each of those kids spent more in a day than I have ever spent in a month. And the parents are just like that. They lie around in the sun a little, but they basically just organize one shopping trip after another. You can see it giving them things to do, filling up the days. What David's parents were really waiting for was dinner time, so they could dress up a little in the clothes they bought, have a lot of drinks, and then go out with their friends to a restaurant for a big dinner, even though there was so much food in the fridge we had to throw it out when we left. They took us kids out a few times, and for the six of us, the bill would come to one hundred and fifty dollars! Two hundred dollars! That's groceries for a week in my house, and we've got thirteen people. And we eat well!"

Tony looked at me uneasily. "So I sound like a creep, don't I, criticizing these people who took me to Florida and gave me a good time. I really did have a good time. But all that buying and spending and shop-ping doesn't do anything for them. Nobody's getting a kick out of anything. David's brothers and sister are the most miserable, whiniest, rudest kids I've ever seen. And as you know, I can be pretty rude myself.

"But there's one thing I know for sure. And I really mean this. If there's one thing I'm going to do for my own kids, it's to make sure they never have a lot of money. I pray to God I don't ever have money. Whatever I do, or whatever becomes of me, I don't ever want to be that way."

* * *

Although Phillip Lithgoe's family was very wealthy, Phillip himself, by spring of his senior year, had lost all possible interest in money. He had only one interest, a consuming interest: Amy Winter, the girl he loved. In my time teaching at the school, I think I have observed every possible manifestation of first love. Boys so stricken are sometimes comical, but more often they are touching. I remember being surprised that boys talk so openly and so well about love. Films tend to portray schoolboys in love as reticent, tongue-tied. The protagonist's friends, and sometimes the protagonists themselves, are leeringly preoccupied with sexual conquest. Limited as my field of observation has been, it is broader than the movie makers', and I will stand by the proposition that boys in school are more romantic than they are horny. Hollywood is mistaken; boys are out primarily for love; they have to be targeted and sold on sex.

Phillip Lithgoe was out for love, and once he found it, he gave himself up ecstatically to the experience. A bright and even a literary boy, Phillip found words for his experience soon after he met and was thereafter transported by Amy. The words were Shakespeare's. Phillip's English class was reading *Romeo and Juliet*, and while the entire play struck resonances in him, one of Juliet's speeches in the first balcony scene stopped him cold:

> And yet I wish but for the thing I have:
> My bounty is as boundless as the sea,
> My love as deep; the more I give to thee,
> The more I have, for both are infinite.

"That's it exactly!" Phillip told me once. 'I wish but for the thing I have.' That's just what I feel the minute I'm not with Amy. I wish for her. I start to worry that something will happen, that I'll lose her—and then I realize that won't happen! I have her. Nothing's in danger. We have each other. It just keeps coming, keeps happening."

Phillip didn't mind at all talking about being in love. Sometimes he seemed fascinated by his own condition, as if it were abstract, separate from him. "It is so good," he would say. "It is so right that it's the thing right is. This has got be be related to health. This is health. This is all you need."

It was nice, by the way, to see Phillip and Amy together. They were both handsome people, and love, as Phillip claimed, seemed to make them paranormally, glowingly healthy. No one observing them for even a moment could fail to see they were in love: loitering against the stadium fence after one of Phillip's track meets or sitting out a dance, somehow communing silently despite the amplified din all about them. To other students, Phillip's and Amy's love transformed the commonplace and made it enviable: Phillip and Amy trying, with too much languor, to learn to juggle; deciding, with too little momentum, where to eat before a movie; walking Amy's dog; studying across a library table from one another; washing a car—it became irresistably desirable to do things like that; to do, really, anything in the company of someone you love so completely.

Phillip was enrolled in my philosophy course, and that spring I had to tell him that a paper he had written comparing naturalistic and idealistic theories of beauty, while not really awful, was far from his best work. He accepted the criticism almost cheerfully. There was nothing at all defensive about his telling me, "You're right, I just wasn't into this one."

He was deeply into the next paper, however. The assignment was to argue for the beauty of some experience: a passage of music, a work of art, a sunset, the lines of a thoroughbred, a smoothly executed golf shot, a double play. Phillip wrote about a particular image of Amy. He chose a moment during their dinner together in a downtown restaurant before the prom. He had just seated her in her place and had returned to his chair facing her. Behind him was a high window through which the setting sun cast a rose-pink wash over the fresh linen on the table and on the white cloth of Amy's dress. She had spent the day outdoors on the water, and the expanses of her cheeks, her brow, her exposed shoulders and throat were rosily flushed as well. The low angle of the sunlight flared and flashed in the silver, in the water goblets, glittered in thousands of facets of the chandeliers overhead. A glitter of white light gleamed from a delicately linked silver chain around Amy's neck. She looked up at him expectantly. There was no sound.

The design of it, Phillip wrote, was overwhelming. It was as if the tufted linen napkins from all the tables were part of a fantastic artificial garden, rosy and peach and perfectly clean. The sun flashing in so much silver and glass heightened the effect, as if uncountable, shivering lights were framing the only living thing in the room: the oval rose and cream of Amy's immaculate head. That it was a sacred night, Prom night, that the dining room was so formally elegant, brightly recalling the history of elegance, the idea of elegance — pulled the moment into esthetic coherence for Phillip.

"I saw what could happen," Phillip wrote. "You could add beauty to beauty and create more. That must be what all great artists do. They don't create beauty out of nothing. They take beautiful things and put them in place. Maybe you have to be in love to do it. Maybe you have to be in love to see it."

* * *

In May of his freshman year, on the last day of track practice, Bobby McLaughlin experienced a moment he has vowed never to forget. Shortly afterward he wrote down an account of it, and he told me once that if he ever had a son, he would tell him about it. Bobby has since left the school, finished college, married and, about a year ago, fathered his first son. Hearing about the son put me in mind of the moment.

Heading along the gravel path that leads from the athletic fields to the house, Bobby found himself trotting side by side with Ahmed Pickett, a senior and the best athlete in the school. Together they slowed to a walk. Bobby's admiration for Ahmed was great, but probably typical of his fellow freshman athletes. Ahmed was a remarkable figure in the school. He was 5'6" and weighed perhaps 150 pounds, but he was extraordinarily well muscled. That fall he had gained more ground and scored more touchdowns than any other running back in Cleveland. He outran defenders in the secondary, but he could also run straight over them on the line. He was a two-way starter, and he played nearly every minute of every game. All eleven opposing players knew where Ahmed Pickett, number 5, was on every play.

Good athletes usually savor a few charged, out-of-time moments: connecting for the home run, sinking the winning basket at the buzzer, breaking loose for the crucial touchdown. Ahmed must have savored hundreds of moments. He never lost a wrestling match. One bitterly raw spring afternoon in a dual track meet he ran the fastest 100-meter dash a schoolboy has ever run in the State of Ohio. The last touchdown he scored for the school was a 95-yard kick-off return in which he broke the tackles of almost every opponent before dashing the final forty yards, seemingly alone. None of my colleagues can remember a more spectacular run. He did it on what our trainer said was the worst sprained ankle he had ever treated.

Physically taut, reserved, well-spoken, Ahmed was the only boy I have known who managed to achieve sustained heroic stature in the school. He had been a weak, problematic student who, with determination and maturity, became a solid one. He was also an excellent chess player, and, while not invincible, was always a match for the most cerebral boys and teachers in the school.

When Bobby McLaughlin found himself alongside Ahmed that warm May afternoon, he did not quite know what to say. But there was something on his mind, something that had been troubling him. Earlier that week, several baseball players were found to have been breaking training. They had been drinking, with the aid of fake I.D.s, at a nearby college bar. The boys, who were prominent members of fall and winter teams as well, admitted to drinking socially all year. "Face it," they told their student judges, "Almost everybody does." The boys were all dismissed from the baseball team, and they forfeited their letters. I heard few complaints about the verdict, but in the aftermath there were complicated sour feelings.

Bobby knew what he wanted to ask Ahmed. "Do you ever drink or do drugs?"

"Nope."

"Have you ever tried them?"

"Nope."

"Why not?"

"Why not?" Ahmed Pickett stopped on the path and squared off opposite the freshman. What he said and the way he said it both scared and thrilled Bobby McLaughlin. "I am an *athlete!*"

* * *

Because I felt I knew him especially well, I agreed to write Tim Stout's official recommendation to college. I had taught him history, served as his faculty advisor, met with his family, and one afternoon after his father's sudden heart attack, sat with him as he shook with grief. His father, Red Stout, had been a larger-than-life figure among the youth of the city. As a young man, he and his college friends created a day camp so action-packed, so eccentric, and so unforgettable that seemingly every boy in greater Cleveland signed up for the summer. At the breakfast hour and again in late afternoon, from June through August, The Red Star Camp's fire engine-red buses streamed through the city's residential neighborhoods. Red Star songs were sung lustily by middle aged accountants and district managers. Red Star pranks and feats were recounted, were worn proudly as badges, by boys over the course of four decades.

Tim was Red Stout's fifth and final son. Tim's big brothers were old enough to be his father, and Tim himself loved to introduce an older nephew to his friends. His friends—and probably half the youth of the city—knew his father Red and his ever-pretty wife Rocky in a way children rarely know other children's parents. To some extent because of this, when Red Stout's heart failed and he died, Tim felt the loss of not only a particular, personal father, but of Fatherhood.

Tim Stout was fifteen when his father died. He grieved, deepened, and grew before our eyes into an admirable and durable young man. Although I planned to work hard on it, his recommending letter to college would be, I felt, blessedly easy to write. The hard letters are those about boys who, while likable and accomplished enough, have indistinct contours, whose lives so far lack story quality. There would be no such problem with Tim. He had been an underskilled, struggling student when he entered the school, but he had battled and prevailed. His math aptitude was so low that, even with earnest effort, he would never, in his algebra teacher's view, make it through the required program. He failed freshman algebra. He repeated it in his tenth-grade year, and by dint of ferocious effort, passed marginally. Not satisfied with his pass, he forfeited a summer of sport and pleasure to take an accelerated algebra review course: three hours of algebra instruction per day, plus five hours of algebra problem-solving outside of class. Immersed in its rules, Tim internalized algebra, and he mastered it, nearly earning an A.

The same drive and tenacity, given his big-boned, well-muscled body, enabled him also to master the conventions of football—but with more instinctive ease. Tim was a complete player, an all-scholastic standout, unanimous captain, school hero. In one game, now enshrined in school memory, he made every one of the team's tackles: every runner, every pass receiver, every punt returner. He is also remembered for single-handedly converting one certain defeat to a storybook victory.

Ahead by two touchdowns with two minutes to play in the game, the opposing team, an arch rival, set up to punt the ball deep in our territory. Our scoring once was unlikely; twice, unthinkable. But Tim, from his linebacker spot, had so battered the opponents' center that on the fourth down, his mind was more on Tim's coming assault than on his snap. The ball sailed far over the punter's head and a hard-rushing end beat the startled punter to the ball, picked it up, and sprinted into the end zone. Still one touchdown ahead,

our rivals executed a slow series of downs, but Tim
threw their runners back jarringly for three consecutive
losses. The opponents back once more in punt forma-
tion, with barely time for another play, Tim again
justified the center's fears by knocking him supine—
but not before another wildly long snap spiralled up
and over the arms of the punter. Like Huns, like Van-
dals, Tim and his fellow defenders pursued the wob-
bling ball, took it on the run, and scored. "Tim wouldn't
accept a defeat," his awestricken coach told the re-
porters afterward. "He just wouldn't accept it."

I watched those games, I knew those stories. I
remembered the passage through his father's loss, the
tenacity in algebra. My recommendation was all but
written. Typically, however, we interview our candi-
dates before we write their letters. The interviews invariably reveal usable details, and they are often a
handy source of quotable opinions and sentiments. It
was always good to talk to Tim, so I arranged a formal
appointment.

When I told him I wanted some background infor-
mation for his college recommendation, Tim winced.
He said he was grateful to me for writing on his behalf,
but he asked if I would do him a favor, and I assured
him I would.

"I would appreciate it," he said, "if you wouldn't
make a big deal out of football. Football's all right, and I
had fun doing it, but that's something I did, not who I
am."

Tim told me he doubted he would play football in
college. When I asked why not, he said he thought he
would be too busy. He said he wanted to study hard in

college, do really well. He decided he had to find a way
to work outdoors for a living, preferably in the wild. He
had talked it over with his brothers, and forestry man-
agement, geology, or agriculture seemed the most
promising courses of study. Pursuing these fields might
mean selecting a college that was off the typical prep-
school graduate's pattern.

I congratulated him on thinking through his future plans so carefully. I didn't admit that I was also
surprised.

"I made my mind up last summer. My brother
helped me find a job collecting data on wolves for a
professor friend of his at Michigan State University. I
spent six weeks, alone most of the time, on a big island
in Lake Superior. My job was to follow the wolves'
migration over the island and to keep records of their
movements and their prey, log the weather, and so
forth. The Michigan State people taught me what to
do, then they left me on my own."

I asked him if he had been scared.

"Of the wolves? No, that's a myth. These were
timber wolves, and they have no predatory interest in
people at all. It's too bad all that business about Little Red Riding Hood and the Big Bad Wolf ever
got started. Wolves in the wild are about as scary as
collies.

"I wasn't scared. I wasn't even lonely. I worked
pretty hard, I think, I got good data, I cooked and
looked after myself, I read two great books, *Heart of
Darkness* and *Moby Dick*, and I started writing a journal, which I have kept going.

"I never felt I was working for a minute. I never

wanted to be somewhere else, to be doing something else. I had no sense of the clock, there was no dividing line between working time and free time. I was just there, figuring things out, learning something every minute. I was so wide awake that the way I am right now is like being asleep compared to it. It was indescribable."

I told him it sounded as if he had had a great summer. Compared to what Tim was telling me and the intensity with which he was talking, my response sounded predictable and dull.

"It was a great summer, but the best part was after I finished on the island. My brother took me on a trip to New England to see the Universities of Maine, Vermont, and New Hampshire. While we were in Vermont, we drove to see this guy who makes birch bark canoes for a living. He makes the most beautiful canoes in the world. He produces every part of them himself. He doesn't use any power tools or electricity. He doesn't use nails or anything from a store. He makes all his own glues and finishes. You should see one of his canoes. They're works of art.

"Talking to him is when it all clicked for me this summer. That guy was doing exactly what he wanted, and it worked. He makes enough from selling his canoes to live, and he doesn't need much. The guy is brilliant. Working with his hands didn't make him stupid, and he seemed totally happy.

"He told us his philosophy. He said the point of building canoes wasn't the canoe when it was finished. The point of building a canoe was building it. The process of building it is the canoe. You had to be, your head had to be in the process, not jumping ahead to the conclusion or how much money you were going to make or what to do with it. It's that kind of thinking that gets people all worked up and drives them crazy. But almost everybody lives that way, and they do poor work.

"He said the point of building the canoe is the building. When you're looking for prime birch, your entire attention is on the search for prime birch. If you're doing that, you will never settle for anything other than prime birch. There are no compromises, no short-cuts. When you're milling the boards, you're doing that, that's your whole business, that's everything. The only outcome is a perfect board; there's no reason for anything less, and there's all the time in the world to do it right. It seems so basic when I talk about it, but it's amazing. You should see one of his canoes.

"So I made up my mind, that's the way I want to live my life. Nothing else makes any sense. I want to do something fine. I want to be totally involved in the doing. As long as I live, I want that awake feeling. Anything else is just kidding yourself."

After talking to Tim, I changed the thrust of my letter recommending him to college. When I finished, my thoughts were still full of his conversation, his experiences on the island and with the canoe-builder in Vermont. Apart from simply admiring Tim, I felt grateful, grateful to be reminded so ingenuously that I too wanted to do something fine, and that that was all I had ever really wanted.

FIVE

After Boyhood

Where be your gibes now? your gambols?
your songs? your flashes of merriment . . .

—Hamlet, V., i.

Disturbing as the notion may be, manhood may be an illusion. That is, the idea of a settled masculine maturity may be an illusion: the sagacious father who knows best, the seasoned, worldly-wise boss, the rock-solid mate, the lifelong friend. Such stereotypes are devised to provide comfort, but they are not quite right, not quite convincing. They derive only feebly from myth, and they do not describe history.

Instead, manhood, by which I mean the cultural face of masculine maturity, may be a husk fashioned to contain and to conceal boyhood. Boyhood does not dissipate or go away; men don't grow out of it. The boy

is always there, needy, insistent, and sometimes ec-
static. Manhood longs for boyhood. Manhood intuits
boyhood, seeks to understand and temper it. Perhaps
the most fully realized maturity a man can attain is the
practical accommodation and consciousness of his own
boyhood.

Denying and suppressing boyhood results in pathology. Social policies suggesting that the genders
should be "blended" into a more unisexual, or completely unisexual, condition deny the inalienable character of boyhood and miss its point. A society may
actually breed what Bly and his therapist sympathizers
call "soft men," but the accommodations they must
make leave these men anxious, unhappy, and ill.

Taken together, the exaggerated posturings of
male pop stars can be seen as a cry of protest against an
incomplete and unfulfilling cultural definition of masculinity. Although they like to promote themselves as
dangerous and mysterious social aberrations, the out-
landish posturing of the likes of Mick Jagger, Aero-
smith, Prince, or Michael Jackson unconsciously confirm what is missing and what is wrong. These figures,
some of them approaching fifty, exclaim their imma-
turity: we are not adults. Nor, certainly, are they men.

Not only is manhood, as popularly understood, an
illusion, it is not even a serviceable illusion. The illusion—father knows best, old shoe, old friend—is un-
helpful because it suggests that dynamic boyhood is
finished, that the male trajectory has reached an end or
has leveled off predictably before its descent into
death. But this is psychologically intolerable. For a
male to acknowledge such a condition is equivalent to

being granted a being of some kind, but no distinctive essence or vitality.

More helpful is the Jungian view, elucidated by James Hillman. According to this conception, the male psyche ranges, over the course of its life span, among and within a number of archetypal possibilities, but two in particular: *puer* and *senex*. *Puer* is pure boy-spirit:

> Its wandering is as the spirit wanders, without attachment and not as an odyssey of experience. It wanders to spend or to capture, and to ignite, to try its luck, but not with the aim of going home. No wife waits; it has no son in Ithaca. Like the senex, it cannot hear, does not learn. The puer therefore understands little of what is gained by repetition and consistency, that is by work ... These teachings but cripple its winged heels, for there, from below and behind, it is particularly vulnerable. It is anyway not meant to walk, but to fly.
>
> ... Instead of psychology, the puer attitude displays an esthetic point of view: the world as beautiful images or vast scenario. Life becomes literature, an adventure of intellect or science, or of religion or action, but always unreflected and unrelated and therefore unpsychological. ... The puer in any complex gives it its drive and drivenness, makes it move too fast, want too much, go too far ... Thus when the puer spirit falls

into the public arena it hurries history along.[21]

Senex is pure old-man spirit:

Personifications of this principle appear in the holy or old wise man, the powerful father or grandfather, the great king, ruler, judge, ogre, counselor, elder, priest, hermit, outcast, and cripple. Some emblems are the rock, the old tree, particularly oak, the scythe or sickle, the timepiece and the skull.

... The temperament of the senex is cold, which can also be expressed as distance. Senex consciousness is outside of things, lonely, wandering, a consciousness set apart and outcast ... He sees the irony of truth within the words, and the city from the cemetery, the bones below the game of skin. Thus the senex view gives the abstract architecture and anatomy of events, plots and graphs, presenting the principles of form rather than connections, interrelations, or the flow of feeling.[22]

The classical myth of Ganymede depicts the puer-spirit. On earth Ganymede is a prince of Troy, who is so beautiful Zeus abducts him and raises him to Olympic status where he serves ambrosial liquors to the court of heaven. Ganymede suggests the masculine condition generally: ascending up and out of the world, an alluring darling to the mature, but never to achieve maturity himself.

Like Jungian archetypes, Plato's concept of pure ideas, or forms, also helps to illuminate the masculine condition. Platonic forms are concepts held to be true by definition. Some, like a right triangle, *pi*, or the C chord, define a highly particular reality. Others, like beauty, cold, or perfection, define more general abstractions. Plato's metaphysical point is that the form is what is true; being immaterial and atemporal, it cannot develop, change or deteriorate. C Chords can be discovered and played, but they cannot be invented; the C chord and every other chord is forever hanging in eternity: pure potential. Youth and maturity may similarly be conceived as Platonic forms. Actual, temporal males may participate in and thus realize these forms for a spell, but it is the fit of person to form that is real and true, not merely the person.

But what of mere persons, mere males? They may feel and even experience consciously the formal requirements of youth and age. They may feel aligned with masculinity itself, but they will never feel formal and abstract; they are alive. Real, living males are for much of their conscious lives hovering between the recollection of boyhood and the fate of boyhood. This is Hamlet. This is Holden Caulfield. The antiheroic condition is to have tasted the drive and the purity of boyhood and then to meditate consciously on the fact that it has no earthly place or use. The anti-hero is acutely sensitive and intelligent. His intelligence tells him that only foolishness and catastrophe lie ahead.

The figure of Hamlet addressing Yorick's skull

represents every male's consciousness of his own earthly condition:

> Where be your gibes now? your gambols? your songs? your flashes of merriment . . .

Yorick had been the palace fool in Hamlet's youth. As such, he had been a kindred spirit. Young Percival too had been a fool, an inspired fool, when he set out weaving his homespun and riding his nag to seek his glory at Arthur's Court. The youthful David is likewise a fool when, against better advice, he stands up to the Philistine champion in the name of the living God; later, to save his outlaw skin, a more worldly-wise David will intentionally act the fool. Here is Francis Bernardone presenting himself naked to his father before all the townsmen of Assisi; Hamlet spouting gibberish to court and kin and fiancée; Holden Caulfield drifting through the human city in the direction of boyhood recalled. Holden's flights of fancy reveal that even he knows how preposterous are the cultural prescriptions for passing into adulthood:

> . . . I hate the movies like poison, but I get a bang out of imitating them . . . all I need's an audience. I'm an exhibitionist. "I'm the goddam Governor's son," I said. I was knocking myself out. Tap-dancing all over the place. "He doesn't want me to be a tap dancer. He wants me to go to Oxford, but it's in my goddam blood, tap-dancing . . . It's the opening night of the *Ziegfeld Follies*." I was get-

ting out of breath. I hardly have any wind at
all. "The leading man can't go on. He's drunk
as a bastard. So who do they get to take his
place? Me, that's who. The little ole goddam
Governor's son."[23]

Not every fool wises up and gets down to tragic
business. Yoricks live on into middle age or old age.
They needn't become as battered and bitter as Lear or
Santiago or old King David. They may simply sustain
their foolishness, like Don Quixote—and in so doing
become something of an inspiration: a holy or heroic
fool, not an anti-hero at all. The costs of heroic foolishness, however, are high; there can be no effective,
sustaining relationships to the practical world or to the
people in it.

Manhood has no happy ending because the masculine trajectory knows no end. Fictions about the
satisfying conclusions of men's lives tend not to work.
They fail to resonate in men's experience and deep
knowing. Thus Dylan Thomas is right to urge his father not to "go gentle into that good night." Lear and
Kurtz and Santiago are not serene. This is not to conclude, however, that masculine experience is inherently tragic or that there is no solace.

There is solace, but it comes from what may seem
to be an unfashionable source, given the psycho-thera-
peutic climate of the late twentieth century. The solace is realized in solitary activity: reflection and medi-
tation. Men require solitude. They need to be alone in
amounts and ways that are probably inherent to their
gender.

In 1988 the British psychiatrist Anthony Storr wrote an extended reflection on the place of solitude in human experience. The book, *Solitude*,[24] attempted to elevate the preference for being alone out of the realm of social aberration and sickness. Drawing on depth psychology, historical example, and clinical research, Storr argues that solitude is essential and good for people. Warming to his thesis, he makes the case that some of society's greatest contributors have lived their lives primarily alone.

> ... many of the world's greatest thinkers have not reared families or formed close personal ties. This is true of Descartes, Newton, Locke, Pascal, Spinoza, Kant, Liebnitz, Schopenhauer, Nietzsche, Kierkegaard, and Wittgenstein. Some of these men of genius had transient affairs with other men or women: others, like Newton, remained celibate. But none of them married, and most lived alone for the greater part of their lives.[25]

Storr set out to write a commentary on solitude, not gender, but the gender implications of his thesis are profound. Only men are included in the list of philosophical solitaries cited above. In subsequent chapters, Storr draws almost entirely on male experience as he documents the adequacy of solitude. The paradigm case is the classical historian, Edward Gibbon, who both lived the solitary life and penned its praises: "Conversation enriches the understanding, but solitude is the school of genius; and the uniformity of a work denotes the hand of a single artist."[26]

Storr's case for the importance of personal solitude inevitably calls into question a good deal of what has become orthodox psychological theory. In Storr's words:

> If we were to listen only to the psychoanalytic "object-relations" theorists, we should be driven to conclude that none of us have validity as isolated individuals. From their standpoint, it appears that we possess value only insofar as we fulfill some useful function vis-a-vis other people in our roles, for example, as spouse, parent, or neighbor.[27]

Storr of course acknowledges the importance, even the survival value, of attachments in human life, especially in the development of children, but he resists the attachment theorists' claim that close personal relationships comprise a kind of hub of human experience and that this hub is the principal source of life's meaning. Attachments are important, useful, and often desirable, but they need not, in Storr's view, become dependencies.[28]

To choose being alone is neither pathological nor anti-social. For Storr, solitude is a developable human capacity. Children, especially loved and secure children, learn to be alone. If they learn it well, then solitude in later life will not be experienced as bad luck or deprivation. Given the trajectory of male experience, the developed capacity for solitude may be a man's only deliverance from despair. Seen this way, being alone is not the cause of isolation and misery; rather, those feelings result from an inability to be alone.

Solitude is not a tragedy. For men it may be salvation from tragedy. Alone, one heals and restores oneself. But solitude is far more than convalescence. In solitude a man, even a very old man, can integrate his boyhood into conscious understanding. Seeing and feeling what boyhood was, what it still is, how it has fit and not fit into practical experience — this is the realization of male maturity. The prophet Elijah, and later Jesus, affirmed their life's work in consequence of forty days' self-imposed solitude. Men tend to worship alone (even amidst crowds). Alone, men are most apt to experience acutely the fit of their own experience into life's context.

Storr sees in Admiral Richard Byrd's 1934 journey to Antarctica a vividly realized quest of meaning through solitude. Byrd did not go to Antarctica because he was unhappy.

> Aside from meteorological and auroral work, I had no important purposes . . . except one man's desire to know that kind of experience to the full, to be himself for a while and to taste peace and quiet and solitude long enough to find out how good they really are.[29]

Byrd's solitary outpost at the South Pole was colder but otherwise not unlike Thoreau's at Walden

Pond. Neither Byrd nor Thoreau was attempting to
escape reality. To the contrary, they were stalking it.
Moreover, in their respective solitudes, both claim to
have found something at once transcendent and real.
Storr cites Byrd's recollection of a solitary walk in the
Antarctic chill:

> Took my daily walk at 4 p.m. today in 89 of
> frost ... I paused to listen to the silence
> ... The day was dying, the night was being
> born — but with great peace. Here were im-
> ponderable processes and forces of the
> cosmos, harmonious and soundless. Har-
> mony, that was it!
>
> ... It was enough to catch the rhythm, mo-
> mentarily to be myself a part of it. In that
> instant I could feel no doubt of man's one-
> ness with the universe. The conviction came
> that that rhythm was too orderly, too harmo-
> nious, too perfect to be a product of blind
> chance ... It was a feeling that transcended
> reason; that went to the heart of man's de-
> spair and found it groundless.[30]

That is not the voice of Lear or the Fisher King.
That is the voice of an actual historical figure, a man of
this century, and it is a voice of ringing affirmation, not
despair. This particular moment of self-realization, of
the fit of self to system, arose for Admiral Byrd when
he was all alone and on his own, questing. That, it
seems, is the way it is with men.

NOTES

1. Sigmund Freud. *Outline of Psychoanalysis*. New York: Norton, 1969, 46-51; "The Passing of the Oedipal Complex," Collected Papers, Vol. II. London: Hogarth Press, 1935, 269-76.
2. Karen Horney. *Feminine Psychology*. New York: Norton, 1973, 133-146
3. Nancy Chodorow. *Feminism and Psychoanalytic Theory*. New Haven: Yale, 1989, 34.
4. Robert Bly. *Iron John*. Reading: Addison-Wesley, 1990. James Hillman. *A Blue Fire*. Robert Moore, ed. New York: Harper and Row, 1989. Robert Johnson. *He!* King of Prussia: Religious Publishing Co., 1974; Robert Moore. *A Blue Fire*. New York: Harper and Row, 1989.
5. Robert Bly. "What Men Really Want." *New Age*, May, 1982.
6. Carl Jung. *Psyche and Symbol*. New York: Doubleday, 1958.

7. Plato. *The Symposium.* Tom Griffith, trans. Berkeley: University of California Press, 1989.
8. Joseph Campbell. *The Hero With a Thousand Faces.* Princeton: Princeton University Press, 1990.
9. Margaret Mead. *Male and Female.* New York: William Morrow, 1949.
10. Quoted in Nancy Chodorow. *Op. cit.,* 34.
11. Erik Erikson. *Childhood and Society.* New York: W. W. Norton, 1985 ed., 102–103.
12. *Ibid.,* 255.
13. Emma Jung, Maria Von Franz. *The Grail Legend.* Boston: Sigo Press, 1986; Robert Johnson. *He! Op. cit.* For a definitive discussion of the sources of Percival's legend, see Jessie Weston's *The Legend of Sir Percival.* New York: AMS Press, 1972.
14. Emma Jung, Maria Von Franz. *Op. cit.,* 300.
15. Robert Johnson. *Op. cit.,* 28.
16. Emma Jung. *Op. cit.,* 155. Here the authors are drawing from the text of *Parzifal* by Wolfram Von Eschenbach, who closely follows Chrétien de Troyes' treatment of the Grail symbols.
17. James Hillman. *Op. cit.,* 228.
18. Robert Bly. *Op. cit.,* 33.
19. Robertson Davies. *The Manticore.* New York: Penguin Books, 1977, 168.
20. Humphrey Carpenter. *Secret Gardens.* Boston: Houghton Mifflin, 1985.
21. James Hillman. *Op. cit.,* 228–230.
22. *Ibid.,* 208–209.
23. J. D. Salinger. *A Catcher in the Rye.* New York: Bantam, 1964, 29.

24. Anthony Storr. *Solitude.* New York: Free Press, 1988.
25. *Ibid.*
26. *Ibid.*
27. *Ibid.*
28. *Ibid.*
29. *Ibid.*35, quoting from Admiral Richard Byrd's *Alone.*
30. *Ibid.*

BIBLIOGRAPHY

Bly, Robert. *Iron John*. Reading: Addison Wesley, 1990.

Campbell, Joseph. *The Hero With a Thousand Faces*. Princeton: Bollinger/Princeton University Press, 1968.

Carpenter, Humphrey. *The Secret Garden*. Boston: Houghton Mifflin, 1988.

Chodorow, Nancy. *Feminism and Psychoanalytic Theory*. New Haven: Yale University Press, 1989.

Davies, Robertson. *The Manticore*. New York: Penguin Books, 1972.

Erikson, Erik. *Childhood and Society*. New York: Norton, 1985.

Freud, Sigmund. *Outline of Psychoanalysis*. New York: Norton, 1969.

Hillman, James. *A Blue Fire*. Robert Moore, ed. New York: Harper and Row, 1989.

Horney, Karen. *Feminine Psychology*. New York: Norton, 1973.

Illich, Ivan. *Gender*. New York: Pantheon, 1982.

Johnson, Robert. *He!* King of Prussia: Religious Publishing Co., 1974.

Jung, Carl. *Psyche and Symbol: A Selection of Writings from C. G. Jung.* Princeton University Press, 1990.

Jung, Emma and Von Franz, Marie. *The Grail Legend.* Boston: Sigo Press, 1986.

Mead, Margaret. *Male and Female.* New York: William Morrow, 1949.

Plato. *The Symposium.* Tom Griffith, trans. Berkeley: University of California Press, 1989.

Salinger, J.D. *The Catcher in the Rye.* New York: Bantam, 1964.

Storr, Anthony. *Solitude.* New York: Free Press, 1988.

Weston, Jessie. *The Legend of Sir Percival.* New York: AMS Press, 1972.

INDEX